It All K
On Sunday

by:
Frank Payne

MAPLE
PUBLISHERS

It All Kicks Off On Sunday

Author: Frank Payne

Copyright © 2023 Frank Payne

The right of Frank Payne to be identified as author of this work has been asserted by the author in accordance with section 77 and 78 of the Copyright, Designs and Patents Act 1988.

First Published in 2023

ISBN 978-1-83538-022-2 (Paperback)
      978-1-83538-023-9 (E-Book)

Book layout by:
    White Magic Studios
    www.whitemagicstudios.co.uk

Book cover design by:
    Haeun Kang

Published by:
    Maple Publishers
    Fairbourne Drive, Atterbury,
    Milton Keynes,
    MK10 9RG, UK
    www.maplepublishers.com

A CIP catalogue record for this title is available from the British Library.

All rights reserved. No part of this book may be reproduced or translated in any form or by any means, electronic or mechanical, including photocopying, recording or by any information storage and retrieval system without written permission from the author.

The views expressed in this work are solely those of the author and do not necessarily reflect the publisher's opinions, and the publisher, as a result of this, disclaims any responsibility for them.

Introduction

At 88 I am still an ardent football fan. I was also a qualified Referee for 42 years, retiring at the age of 72, sixteen years ago. From ten-year-olds to sixty-five-year-old veterans' sides. Every weekend. Strictly applying the laws of the game, I vowed to uphold. No matter what age the teams. I truly loved what I did. And for 42 years I did it well.

What I witnessed during the last European Cup saddened me. The failure of referees to apply those same rules, particularly when England's young team played Denmark and Italy. Both referees ignored the letter of the laws they swore to uphold. In my opinion, having spent most of the game kicking the opposition, Italy should have been disqualified for continually trying to intimidate the opposition.

Especially in the final. Having gone a goal down in two minutes, it was blatantly obvious they intended to intimidate the young English team. The only good thing I can take from that game. Despite being almost kicked off the park. The young team refused to retaliate. The greatest sadness of all is that there were no official complaints raised.

Once qualified, the laws sensibly applied, filled the next forty-two years of my life with cheers, tears and fears. Leaving a loyal disciple of the beautiful game a sadly frustrated, disappointed ex-referee. A cabinet full of memories. Both good and bad. But far too many bad. My whistle and flags, necessary disciplinary aids when sensibly used.

Without football's laws, applied as intended, referees could not have game control. And without a referee's control, the beautiful game would no longer be.

Chapter One

From the age of eight I fell in love with Football. At the age of eighty-eight I'm still in love with the beautiful game. I stopped playing through injury, at twenty-three. Just one year before I surrendered my freedom and married. Foolishly and without informing Pat of my intentions. Once married, instant pregnancy with boy child was the order of the day. Of the birth of a girl child, once again instant pregnancy would follow. Eventually I was able to persuade the Stork Delivery Service to provide positive help in delivering the much-wanted boy child. However, I refrained from complaining. It was fun trying.

At last, here he was. Ashley, the object of my continual want. England's future brilliant goal scoring machine. My passport to fame and fortune. But one's best laid plans do oft times gurgle down the toilet. Mine did. But not before I had spent the next forty something enjoyable years in love with the beautiful game. And all because I was ambushed by an eight-year-old brat. The fruit of my loins who stopped playing pretence football when he left the Cubs.

No sooner had Christopher, my eight-year-old son returned home from his weekly Cub pack night, the tears came in torrents. Normally he couldn't wait to tell his mother and me all about the night's activities. But not tonight. Even before removing his toggle, he burst into floods of tears. Having no idea what was wrong, or had happened during the pack meeting, I was immediately alarmed. When the tears had subsided, he told me.

Just before the evening ended, the pack leader told them the football team coach and manager said he'd had enough, and he was packing it in. As of now he would take them to the weekend game but no further. If a dad, big brother, sister, or family relative would not volunteer to take the team further, then any future cub football would be kicked into touch. A thing of the past.

Once more the chin began to quiver, and the tears mix with the Mars bar. A bribe to stop the tears. Crammed into his mouth in the hopes a second would follow. It was proffered and tear cessation followed. I asked how many cubs were there in his pack. Christopher answered twenty-three. "Surely Chris," I said. "One of their dads or big brothers would jump at the chance of managing a bunch of super-stars like you." I then went on to say that if nobody put his or her name forward, then tell Mr. Arkwright I'll do it. But only short term until a new coach/manager volunteered.

Did I or did I not perceive a look of triumph appear momentarily on his tear sodden face? It was there, I swear, as he bade me goodnight. Bounding up the stairs, two at a time before I could question him further. I didn't know it then, but I had been well and truly conned. Ambushed, which I only knew that weekend. When Mr. Arkwright came calling after his game on Saturday. Laden with arms full of muddied football kit, linesman flags, first-aid kit. Plus, would you believe, a whistle! To say I was surprised would be an understatement. On first sight of the mud-filthy kit, Pat, my wife was apoplectic. My wee sod of a son, flushed with success. But I must truthfully admit, football for me, with all its club coaching, team management and referee trials and tribulations started right there and then. But please don't tell Chris. If ever he found out, he'll demand repayment of his three month's pocket money. Stopped because I do not appreciate being taken for a mug. By anybody, especially my eight-year-old son. Who when Mr. Arkwright announced there would be no more football, told me it was Chris's hand immediately raised first, accompanied by, "My dad's looking for something to do at weekends." I think you'll agree, as an eight-year-old, he was destined to be a politician.

The next Cub pack meeting provided me with the first opportunity of meeting the team I had unknowingly, and begrudgingly inherited. What I saw and heard left me far from enthusiastic. As did the season's results. Games played six. Games won nil. Games drawn nil. Games lost six. Goals scored four. Goals conceded sixty-seven. The only thing they had in shed loads was enthusiasm. Despite score lines like 21-1 (the one being an own goal). When I asked who the players were, all 23 little hands shot heavenwards. The problems I faced seemed insurmountable. As indeed proved the case when we played our first game under the guise of new management. Me.

It was wet, cold, windy and ankle deep in mud. Almost knee deep for our smallest players. There were no changing facilities. The team on the opposite side of the pitch were twice our size. So big I asked their manager if they were on the right pitch. When he said they were I wanted to pack it in. There and then. Award the game to opponents. Go home and forget all about being a cub football team manager. When the fifth goal went in, six minutes into the first half, I wish I had. The only time our goalkeeper touched the ball was to pick it out of the back of the net. By half time we were down to nine players. Why? Not for foul play. Violent conduct. Foul and abusive language. Violation of any of the laws of the game. No. Their mothers thought enough was enough. Walked on to the pitch. Picked them up and took them home. We lost 17-0. Inwardly my heart and soul wept in unison. Cried out resign. You're on a hiding to nothing. For as long as you're in charge.

I drove home in silence. Chris and a few of the team my passengers. One of them, Gary Jones by name. One of the few who tried very hard throughout the game. I felt his small hand on my shoulder. "Sorry Mr. Payne," he said. Then, with conviction went on, "We tried, but if you help us, I know we'll get better. I promise." I knew then I could not turn my back on such an earnest plea. It was going to be painful, difficult, often disappointing and above all else, unrewarding. For long periods at a time. But could there be success before cubs became scouts? Coupled with Jones's promise, who was I to walk away? Talking to other cub team managers, I realised why there were very noticeable differences in size and stature between the teams. Those playing in ours were mainly first year cubs. Whilst a few were second year. Our opposition were the very opposite. Almost without exception, most of the opposition were just months away from becoming scouts. The difference therefore in height, weight and football playing experience was decidedly the reason for the huge defeats we were suffering, whenever we played. But still my team of mighty midgets kept coming back for more. Once I realised how huge the disadvantage was, my mind was made up. Forget the remainder of this season. And probably the next. I had already decided if we were to win medals, it would be in the final year they remained cubs. The first decision made in the many years which followed, managing boys' football clubs.

Chapter Two

Me and Jonesy. A partnership formed in the back of my car, returning home after one more devastating defeat. One which developed over the next eight years. Me aged thirty. Gary aged eight. The nearest father and son relationship that was 'not of the blood'. It could well have been as Jean, his Mum, was a delightfully ambassadorial lady. I had asked Mr. Arkwright if I could address the cub pack, to which he readily agreed. There were cheers when I told them I was pleased to be asked to manage the football team. I then told them that I was no pushover. I would only accept those who genuinely loved and wanted to play the game. Improve as they played. Like me, give up each Saturday morning. Snow, rain, shine. Mud or flood. Train hard, work hard. Focus, listen and learn. I had written a letter for each of their parents. Informing them why, when and where I would need their support. With both the boys and most of the parents agreeing to my terms, we were on our way. So, what now needed to be done? Send a warning to Alex Ferguson. The then manager of Manchester United, the team of the decade. "Watch out Fergie, we're coming to get you." My team of mighty midgets thought that was cool. It confirmed they knew I meant business.

It was Saturday morning. The first of our new training sessions would begin on Langton's school football pitch today. Most of the cubs went to this Hornchurch school. I worried through breakfast just how many of the cubs would keep their promise and be there. I needn't have worried. Not only was it a full house, but many of their dads also accompanied them. We were in business. I had also invited a work colleague to join me. He was still playing high level team football. I needed his help and opinion. I had also asked him to bring along some of his clubs training balls, which he also did, ten in total. Bob was a rave. He took the whole pack right back to basics. How to kick the ball with maximum power and distance. Kill and control a moving ball. Judge the weight of passing the ball to his other team players. The boys loved every minute. As did the dads, some of whom joined in the passing game. Played in the final fifteen minutes of training. It proved beyond doubt, every parent there could see I was taking my managerial duties seriously.

We trained every Saturday in between the final three cub league games left, before the season ended. We managed a draw in our final game, giving the opposition a nasty fright. Other managers accused me of having other than registered cubs in the team. I must admit it had once crossed my mind, watching twenty feet hurtling after the same ball. Sometimes twenty-two when the goalkeeper, losing it completely, threw caution to the wind, rushing wildly out of his goal to join in the free for all. However, once Bob arrived, turning 'rookies' into football focused players became the immediate priority, if we were to succeed. We worked hard once the cub games ended. Whilst Bob took training whenever he could, he left us with loads to practice in his absence. Slowly the boys improved beyond my expectations. They physically grew taller, heavier, tougher, and far more skilled in their footballing endeavours. Before their involvement with cub footballing ended, they were cup finalists in the third season Then won the league and cup double in their final year. It was then, and only then, I thanked Chris, my son, on bended knee for his perfect ambush. He had little recollection of that fateful evening. In truth he believed I had blown a head gasket.

When I first came on the scene, my fondness for the squad of first year cubs I had inherited, was apparent in the name I bestowed upon them - "Langton's Babes in Football Boots." The training was tough for ones so young. Intentional, intended to sort the boys from the babes. It did, whether in training or matches. Often in adverse weather conditions. Even when it was colder than a witch's tit. Sometimes both. So, by the time cub football ended, we were ready for local league football. And all that entailed. To my heartfelt relief, the whole team decided to stay together. All that is bar one. Gary Sparkes. His elder brother played for Gidea Park. An excellent, successful, and well organised club who usually were amongst the honours at the finish of each season. Gary was one of my best players whom I could ill-afford to lose. But as I soon discovered, poaching other club players were rife in boys' football. Even at this age level, bribery occurred. Cases I could prove where money was involved. But more often than not, it was tours abroad. Even to the USA as well as Europe. Now, it was no longer simply gathering eleven boys together and turning up for the game. Oh dear me no. We needed a regular pitch, two sets of kit, balls for training and matches, indoor winter training facilities and League joining fees. Above all else we needed money. Quite a substantial amount. Now it was the parents' turn to really become involved in Langton Royals. The name finally and unanimously agreed upon.

Peter Webber, the dad of one of my star players, Stephen, had been my second-in-command throughout four years of cub football. Right through to the prospect of signing as a new local league team. From day one, his support given readily and without reservation, was invaluable. I doubt there would ever have been a Langton Royals without

Peter's colossal input. It was he, who without my prior knowledge, set up a parents' meeting with a one-word agenda. MONEY!

I thought it only right and proper to allow him to run the meeting. With help from me when called upon. For me there was an important decision to be made. Do I call it a day and retire with two years of triumphant cub football on my sport CV? Or use this as a solid base to carry on and win more silverware? I thought I'd know when tonight's meeting ended.

Seventeen parents of the cub squad players were invited to the meeting. All attended, assuming I would carry on as manager. Peter had done his homework, regarding what Langtons faced as a new team, joining any one of several local boys' club Leagues. Including an annual fee of twenty pounds for each Langton player. This to cover the cost of two full playing strips. The cost of pitch and indoor training facilities. Organising fund raising events, including dinners, dances, raffles, table-top sales, and the like. Would the mums agree to share washing muddy playing kit? Also, who would take on perhaps the most important role in the Club's future? That of Treasurer. Two dads volunteered and both were appointed. Believing where money was concerned, two heads were better than one. That's when I rose to my feet, telling the assembled gathering I would be honoured to continue as manager. I could do little else after such an eager, excited, and supportive reaction from those present. Within days, a whole string of money ideas was on the table.

Chapter Three

I was extremely lucky when Peter suggested I take a look at the Langton school team, for whom several of the cubs played. He said they were a good young team. He'd heard players' dads suggest they were strong enough to stay together after they left Langton's for senior school. I respected Peter's opinions. Also, his suggestions that there were players who he believed would strengthen our existing squad. He had previously mentioned me and our existing cub squad to some of those dads. And his fears that the cub team was not strong enough, as did I, if we were to succeed in the transition to any of the local soccer leagues. As I had previously said, I could and did totally rely on his judgement. So, I agreed for him to arrange a meeting with those dads, who had voiced the wish that the Langton squad stayed together.

I knew Peter well enough to expect a pub would be the venue. He knew his Langton team dads would love his choice. So, pub it was and a full house in attendance. Better still quite a few of the mums came too. Having been introduced, to keep the meeting light, tight and friendly, I asked the mums with washing machines to hold up their hands. Why? I told them I would produce a roster for kit washing after each game. Not one of those lovely mums complained. Neither then, nor throughout each season. Peter then went through the requirements of a newly formed league team. There were surprises at what was required. Not unexpected. But happily, hardly one word of dissent. As the cub team grew bigger and more physical, so did their matches. Along with the behaviour of parents and supporters. Fortunately, Peter and I were able to control the more vocal of ours.

Strangely enough it was Gary Jones, the team captain's dad, who was the worst offender. He kept up a non-stop barrage of pointed and loud abuse directed at both the opposition players and parents. Eventually, all my efforts having failed to quieten him, I enlisted the help of Jonesy. It worked a treat. But there was a niggle beginning to gnaw at me. Growing season by season. As games increased physically, so did the visible seeds of violence. Both verbally and, occasionally, physically. Often because the younger players' matches were rarely blessed with that all-important man-in-black. The referee. Like me, lovers of the beautiful game will be shocked to discover that should Essex FA recruit 150 referees in a season, they will have lost 100 by the season's end. Why? They will as one man tell you. Refusing to give up Saturday, Sunday, or both. Paid a miserly fee if you did. Being sworn at, spat at, violently threatened, and altogether humiliated. When all they wanted was to enjoy the game. Whilst doing their level best to ensure players, managers, parents, and supporters did too.

As Langton Royals, our five first new Belhus and District League games were without league appointed referees or linesmen. During the league briefing, we were told should this happen, ask the away opposition manager if he, or one of his dads would referee the game. If not, either you or one of your dads should do it. Under no circumstances can the game be allowed to proceed without a referee. Next, two linesmen need to be appointed. One from each side. However, this is not obligatory. The game can proceed without them. As a referee, I have now and again needed to dismiss mine. Usually, because of incompetence, lack of knowledge of the laws of the game or bias. But, and the most annoying. Failure to comply with my instructions, given before the game began. But never dismiss them if league appointed. Which is usually for cup games. Perhaps you are now beginning to better understand why there is all too often player ill-discipline in boys' and youths' football. Together with out-and-out violence in adult games. Sadly, I further believe it's on the increase.

As I said previously, we had not a single referee appointed to our first five games, only one of which was taken by the opposition manager. Now I know I could have handled the other three better. But If I wasn't very good, he wasn't either. Not only were too many of his decisions unfair. He was blatantly biased. If our start to league football was far from satisfactory, so was the behaviour of Stan Jones. His violent outbursts during our very first game included, "You've still got last year's mud on your bleeding boots, I'd like to stick that bleeding whistle up your arse, where it belongs," "When are you going to open your bleeding eyes as well as your bloody mouth?" " 'Ave you got bleeding lead in your flag?" This to the opposition linesman. Neither Peter, I or any of the mums or dads could shut him up. At the end of our first Belhus league season, I understand why Jones's mum never came to a game. Nary a one. But I had made a decidedly important decision. Before the start of next season, I would become a qualified referee. And I did. Then, as a referee, if he continued harassing players, parents/supporters. Me too. I could and would ask him to leave the game, ban him from the touchline, threaten to abandon the game. Send an official report to the league referee's secretary to deal with. They could, and probably would fine the club to boot. Whilst he didn't appreciate it at all when this was explained to him, "fermez la grande bouche" won the order of the day.

Finishing sixth in a league of fourteen club teams, we acquitted ourselves well in our first match. I learned a lot, as did the boys. We were confident and knew, with Jonesy as Skipper- and his dad no longer a touchline menace - improvement would come. For those readers who do not know or remember, football then was nothing like it is today. On the pitch and during the game, both sides stuck rigidly to what was called the " W " formation. Beyond the goalkeeper were two defenders, namely left and right full backs. Directly in front of them were three half backs, positioned right across the park. They would also act in defence if and when their goal was threatened. Their key role however was to support the five forwards. Then the game was fast flowing, often resulting in goals, with the game moving swiftly end to end. My then first division team were Charlton Athletic. I've stood on the terraces, witnessing a London derby with over 60,000 mixed Charlton and Arsenal supporters in the Valley. A ground I understood had a capacity of over 72,000 fans. Charlton won 5-4. Lots of rival banter but never ever a punch thrown in anger. Sadly, that couldn't and wouldn't happen today.

Sitting the Referees examination's six-week course, I realised how little I really knew of all the laws of the game. The course tutor was a pro of 40 years standing. After the first session I vowed I would be as good as him. Perhaps not in applying those rules but matching him in time spent in my blacks. I'd set my application of the rules out separately for adult and junior games. Mainly because the length of playing time was differently upwards of 15 minutes. At the end of my third season as a qualified ref, I decided to finish with the adult game and concentrate on boys' football. Taken after I witnessed reckless violence whilst officiating at a friendly. It was a Sunday when Langton Royals' game was postponed due to flu running riot in the opposition's camp. I was contacted by a colleague. He felt rough and asked if I could run the game for him. Knowing he would do the same for me, I readily agreed.

It was a two o'clock kick off on Sunday. The ground was a forty-minute drive from my home. It was blowing a mini gale and halfway there the heavens opened. I arrived thirty minutes early to run my normal pitch markings, both goals and nets, players' kit and boot inspection. All passed muster. I had however noticed there was a pub on the opposite side of the road. And there was a strong smell of alcohol in the home side's dressing room. As neither wind nor torrential rain had abated, I asked both skippers if they wanted to postpone the game. They said no, but I swear I noticed a hint of malice as the away team manager said, "We've waited a bloody long time for this." Deep down, alarm bells started to softly ring. As I tossed the coin to decide ends, a little voice in my head kept repeating, "This is going to a toughie." It was, and friendly or not I abandoned it after seventy minutes of physical violence and football mayhem.

Chapter Four

The pitch was ankle deep in mud, which obliterated many of the necessary pitch markings. This was bad news for both club linesman and me. As if that wasn't enough, when I called both linesmen over to give them my instructions, neither could stop glaring at each other. Neither paid attention, as I discovered within ten minutes of the game getting underway. Each had only one thought in mind. To get as many opposition players sent off as was humanly possible. The first bout of fisticuffs broke out in the sixteenth minute. I didn't see how or why it began. I was down-field keeping up with play, my back to the incident. Normally I could have relied on my linesman's report. But not the two I had today. Both were so biased I dare not rely on anything they thought they saw, or said. Consequently, after yellow carding both players, I dismissed both linesmen there and then, despite disagreement from both managers, who were playing and captaining the dockers' and pub sides. In the three seasons I had been officiating at adult games, I'd earned the name of "Red Frank". Why? Because in my opinion, the number of sending offs was in keeping with the offences committed. In this instance, I could not send the two players off as I did not see the incident. Nor believed one word of what the linesman said, leading up to punches being thrown. Later a neutral spectator told me the pub player had called the docker "a fucking wanker," long after he'd punted the ball downfield. He then used two hands to push the pub player over, who got up and swung a punch, which missed. Then fisticuffs were threatened, cheered on by supporters on both sides of the pitch. I knew then my life was in danger. Also, had I known this "friendly" was in fact a long-standing war of attrition, built upon five years of bad blood, I would have straightway declined the fixture. The cause, a reckless tackle in the very first fixture, five years ago, which resulted in a broken leg. I called both captains to the centre circle and loudly addressed them in language they could not but clearly understand. It made not one jot of difference. We were now halfway through the second half with the scores level at two each. And I had just dismissed my third player for spitting. After yellow carding seven players from both sides, I'd truly had enough. I thought, sod this game, I'll be diplomatic. There's twenty minutes to full time, the score is 2-2. I've sent players off from both sides. I'm still sound in life and limb and intend to keep it that way.

I strode purposefully to the centre, blew three blasts long and loud on the whistle. The game stopped dead. All players' heads turned to me. I had the stage to myself. So, I started. "I am abandoning the game now, before anybody gets seriously hurt. The score is tied so nobody loses. Although I'm right in saying football does. You didn't come here to play. Only to cause as much damage to each other as you possibly could. Had this been a league game I would have abandoned it long before half-time. If you intend carrying on, you have twenty minutes left to play. But I won't take any further part in this travesty I have witnessed today. You are a disgrace to the game." With that I headed back to the changing rooms. Fully expecting to be accosted and threatened before I reached the safety of the referees' dressing quarters. I looked back momentarily to see they had restarted the game. Giving me time to be changed and gone before the game ended. Before reaching my car,

I wondered should I risk my life before going back for my fee!

Driving home I was angry and soul searching. I should, in all honesty, have abandoned the game well before half-time. But I didn't. And by not doing so, I encouraged it all to kick-off on Sunday. There and then I decided to remove my name from all Essex adult leagues available referees' lists. Concentrate purely at officiating boys' football only. Girls' football too, but that was a long, long way off in the 70's. I further decided to write to Essex FA, detailing events as they had happened. Asking them to warn all listed referees to refuse to officiate at any future adult fixtures involving either or both teams. Incidentally and totally unbeknown to me, some adult teams whose games I had refereed, had given me the name "Red Frank". Whilst I thought this harsh, I think it acted as a warning to those teams known to play to their rules, not the FA's.

Finally let me close this chapter on a sad but true occurrence. It concerns a seventeen-year-old youth, whose father persuaded him to become a referee. He took the exams and passed. From now on his would be an important role in the game he loved. Six months later he gave up. I tried to reason with him, but his mind was made up. He said, "Why should I give up Sunday, the only day I get off, to be sworn at, spat at, threatened, hit by thrown coins, pushed and punched?" I had no arguments left. You've probably guessed by now, that referee was my seventeen-year-old son.

There were other unwholesome reasons I red-carded myself from all adult league referees' lists. I witnessed a player chasing the referee, knife in hand which he had hidden in his sock. Fortunately, the referee was far quicker than the player. I was asked to give evidence at the tribunal, which I did. The player was banned, sine die, and arrested on a criminal charge. His club fined and dismissed from the league. I heard later it had finished with football altogether. In another incident, a silver haired, elderly referee came into the dressing room just as I was leaving. He had obviously had a bad game. He slumped, visibly upset, on the bench, and angrily said, "The bloody league failed to appoint linesmen for my bloody game." Being a cup quarter-final they were obliged to do so. He'd just finished telling me this, when a very angry supporter of the losing team burst into the ref's partitioned part of the dressing room. He grabbed the elderly referee by his black tunic and slammed him up against the wall, all the time shouting, "You fucking useless prick. You've just cost us the fucking cup."

Although in shock, I leapt to my feet, rushed across the gangway and grabbed the intruder around the neck. By this time, the old boy was shouting, "It wasn't my fault, it wasn't my fault." Fortunately, other players from this game were entering the dressing room, saw what was happening and helped me prise the intruder off him. They held the angry supporter till he calmed down, finally making him understand the referee was right. The league had not appointed the necessary linesmen and because it was bitterly cold and there were few supporters, nobody volunteered to run the line for him. The old chap offered to postpone the game, which both sides refused. So, it went ahead, without linesmen. They would have been able to compensate for the elderly referee's lack of pace, being unable to keep up with play. This is vital for any referee. I know not what happened on this occasion, but usually the league escapes punishment. Sadly, clubs and players rarely do. Because of the nature of the amateur game, incidents are no stranger. Fortunately, events, when they happen, both punishable and amusing, usually happen in equal number. Or so it seemed to me in junior soccer. Like most referees at senior level, I've been deliberately pushed, manhandled, spat at, sworn at, hit by thrown plastic water bottles, bundled to the ground, warned to keep looking over my shoulder, threatened and hand bagged. Whilst this went on all the time I officiated in senior football, such incidents lessened dramatically when my refereeing was concentrated on the junior game. If any of you wonder why, let me explain. Because of the playing ages concerned, I was inclined to be more lenient. The reason why is summed up in one word - INTENT. Yes of course intent is visible in junior games. But it has a far different interpretation. And if you are an intelligent referee, you'll quickly come to understand what that meaning is. Almost at every level of adult amateur league football, money is involved when you play. Added to which there is often win/draw bonuses. Also, the pride in your league position. So, you, as a player are intent on winning every game. No matter who gets hurt. Today, physicality and the professional foul has become an integral part of soccer, encouraged, or so I am led to believe, by most managers. Stop the other team playing would probably be his last instruction, as his team took the field.

The very simple intent of junior teams is to win. For each player to become a better player. Improve with every game played. Most fouls by seniors are intentional. By juniors accidental. Although, as a referee, you will begin to see this change when players reach youth level. If you are a good referee, you'll be watching out for this and act accordingly.

Chapter Five

I said earlier in my time as the man in black. I recall incidents, both amusing and against the laws of the games I religiously upheld, which were fairly even. Before I sat the referee's exam, I would officiate in cub games if nobody else held up his or her hand to do so. The match to which I refer was an under nine league match but not involving my cub team. There was one player who obviously had no wish to be on the park. His interests were one hundred percent elsewhere. As we lined up for kick-off, I noticed his right bootlace was undone. A danger if left that way. Telling him to do it up, I then started the game. As it progressed, every time I passed the centre circle there he was. In the same spot. As if, like a flower, he'd been planted. He just never moved, even though I told him several times to join in the game. Finally, now fed up with telling him and having run out of patience, I stopped and shouted, "Get your laces tied, you little bugger." Whereupon another boy, even smaller, ran up to me and said, "If my mum heard you say that she'd have taken me off." I was speechless. Later in my years as a referee, I had in three league/cup games, officiated for the same Essex team. They were a good if physical side who, in their play, just now and again erred on the wrong side of right. I often wondered if they knew of my tag of Red Frank. I respect physical, if fairly and properly adopted. During play, and perhaps to intimidate the opposition, it too often wasn't. I let them get away with nothing. In the three games to date, I had yellow carded seven of the Dagenham players and sent two off. One for using foul and abusive language and the other, violent conduct. I was number one football enemy to the players. More so to their supporters who normally totalled 100 plus. I had needed to remonstrate with them on three different occasions. I was allocated their home game at the request of the home side. Knowing our history over past seasons, I was both surprised and suspicious.

The official dressing rooms were a considerable distance from the pitch. I arrived early to inspect the pitch for correct pitch markings, goalposts and nets. They were sound. Everything was fine, so it was back to the referees' changing room. Knowing the game was going to be fast, competitive, physical and no doubt eventful. While getting changed into my blacks and checking my kit, I wondered how many supporters would be present. And again, whether the usual reception would be received when I appeared. But why had they asked for me? Little did I know, so I gave myself plenty of time to walk the few hundred yards to the pitch. As I got closer, I reckoned there were over 150 supporters. But on this occasion, why so silent? Normally I would arrive to a barrage of ribald comment. But I was soon to find out why it was absent. When I reached the centre circle, I heard a shout, "Hey ref. " I turned to face the Dagenham crowd. As I did, they, as if to a man, stamped down on their left foot, thrusting their clench fisted right arm high in the air in salute as they did so, bellowing, "Sieg Heil – Adolph's Back," in unison. Grinning, I answered with a reversed two fingered Churchillian war time V salute. The players were all aged sixteen. Physicality was now an acceptable part of their game. I therefore needed to get hold of the game from the start. Which I did, letting nothing go which would later lead to trouble. It was a good game ending in a 2-2 draw. A fair result with only one booking necessary. I was delighted, recalling bookings/sending offs made in previous games handled. More pleasing was being told 'I'd had a good game' by both managers. A rare occurrence indeed.

Driving home, I realised there was a growing difference in pace now needed to keep up with youth games. Quite noticeable for elderly refs like me. In one other Romford under 15's game, I was late due to a traffic accident. I went straight to the dressing rooms. It was a school pitch where players/referees shared the same facilities. I went quietly to the back of the room. Standing in front of me, shielded by hanging clothes, was a boy named Shaun. I knew him from the previous game, where I threatened to book him for dissent. A busy player, one who loved to talk. Then the team sheet came round which he had to sign. On it was my name as referee. Shaun turned to his teammate and said, "Frank Payne, isn't he that grey haired, bearded, old bastard who looks like Father Christmas we had a few weeks ago?" That's when I said, "Good morning, Shaun, looking forward to the game." I said nothing else, but knew he knew I'd heard what he'd previously said.

About 15 minutes into the game, I found him running beside me. He started to apologise and begun by telling me I was a good ref. I cut him short and said, "No Shaun, you're right. I am that grey haired bearded bastard who looks like Santa. But you're also wrong. He's nice. I'm not. I'm a nasty bugger. Put one foot wrong and I'll prove it. Now get on with the game," which they lost 3-2.

Of all the admonishments I handed out in the 40 years I remained a referee, one stands out. It happened during a sixteen-year-old boy's fixture. Within minutes of starting the game, a home side player opened his mouth when he was penalised. It then remained open till half-time. Almost every decision I gave against his side, he loudly queried. Having warned him to keep it shut, he didn't. So, I yellow carded him for dissent just before half-time. I had no option when, early in the second half, penalising his team, he very loudly said, "You on their fucking side ref?" At half time I had asked their manager to talk to him or his team would be down to ten men. Before starting the second half I also called him to me and sternly warned him he would be red carded for one more vocal outburst directed at me. He glared at me as he walked away. Within minutes he deliberately tripped a rival player. That was it, as well he knew. I called him to me. He didn't move and shouted, "Fuck off." I went to confront him, reaching for my notebook and red card. Slightly off balance he pushed me hard with both hands to my chest. I hit the ground forcibly as he started to walk away. It would have been foolhardy for me to have followed. Before restarting the game, I told the manager he was being sent-off for dangerous play. My report to the league would give full details of his conduct throughout the game. Plus, my half-time warning to his team manager. I gave evidence at the tribunal and at the age of sixteen, he was banned sine die from league football. His club were also fined and warned as to their, and their players', future conduct.

In all the official league referee meetings, there would always be reports of similar incidents occurring. Fortunately, because I had decided to concentrate eighty percent of my active refereeing time officiating youth football games I was rarely physically threatened or abused. But yes, I have been spat at, kicked and physically threatened. Sadly, the same cannot be said of practising adult senior referees. Here, physicality was an all too often practised part of the senior game. What I fail to accept is why league officials, dealing with various degrees of physical retaliation, seem all too willing to also penalise the official. This, when, if we recruit 150 referees in a year, we lose 100 of them. I believe the above figure would noticeably change. With referee shortage an annual recurring serious football problem, it's one that needs all the help it can get. In all my whistle blowing days, to me it was important to remember the vows I made, to officiate by them. Perhaps more leniently in young games, where I took the opportunity to carefully and verbally explain why I had penalised the player. This I always explained to both managers prior to kick off. They were pleased to give me the authority to go ahead. Never once, in my forty odd years, did I receive one player objection.

Sadly I have watched the current laws of the game being ignored time after time after time. No matter what level of competition involved. Even shouting loudly at the man in the middle when his decision (or no decision too often) makes mockery of the rules. I strongly believe money is the reason football's disciplines are being all but ignored.

For me it came to a head during the 2020 European Cup. I became so incensed I wrote a letter following Italy's stolen victory. It was sent to leading national newspapers. Whether or not it was published I don't know. Only that I did not receive one reply. But then, when managers of the Premier Division clubs are heard saying of dangerous opposition players, "Don't let him play," or referees being told to "let the game flow" by those in authority, I'm not surprised.

Chapter Six

Langton Royals were now in their fourth Belhus League season. We were also top of the table with just three more games to play. Unless anything untoward happened, we would finish under-14 league champions. We were also in the league cup final. It was a double we could and should win. We did, easier than expected, with the score 4-1 in our favour. They were in fact the first team we ever played in youth league football. Strangely, we were then beaten 4-1. Revenge is mine, sayeth the Lord. In all games so far between us we had each won, drawn, and lost, two. Their manager had promised new track suits if they won the cup-final, but they didn't. In my and Peter's opinion, there were few, in fact very few teams who would have beaten us, the way we played that day. We were brilliant. I was later told, having lost the game, he totally lost it altogether, threatening to give up his management, whilst pretending to jump up and down on his boy's new track suits. Bought especially for the cup final he was convinced they would win.

The reward for us, the winners. We told the team in the dressing room after the match euphoria had died down. We were going to Spain for a three-day tour at Easter. On hearing this, euphoria erupted again. But this time the volume had trebled. We heard after all delayed league games had been played, the other cup finalist remained league runners-up, on goal difference. They had however lost their last game. In a fit of pique, their manager was seen jumping up and down on those new and personalised cup final track suits. He was so convinced they would win the cup and league double. Football. It can be a funny old game! With league and cup final double trophies, highly polished by proud mums, taking pride of place in our virgin trophy cabinet. We had now made a promise to the team we had to keep. Once again money raised its insatiable head. Taking an estimated party of 40-50 adults and fourteen-year-olds to Spain at Easter was a formidable task. One we had to confront head-on.

So we did. Within days, a "money for Spain" emergency meeting was called, inviting ideas from the mums and dads who would be accompanying the team. After lengthy deliberations and by a narrow margin we settled on organising a grand dinner dance. At the Upminster Country Club who carried the vote unanimously. Although all present knew it would be a tall order to fill its 400 capacity. We just about had time to do it if everyone present gave it their best shot. They did. One hundred and ten percent plus. We had a full house with two weeks to spare. With the club agreeing to pay for the team, and parents paying their own way, it was one of those occasions where everything went swimmingly. The band, in which Eddie, one of the players' dads who played saxophone, were superb throughout the evening. Plus, thanks to his influence, they charged half their normal fee. Our local M.P. was guest of honour. In a humorous twenty minute after dinner speech, he revealed some of the behind the scenes and Westminster antics we never get to see or hear about. Just about everybody was keen to dance, having enjoyed an excellent four course meal. We were all surprised when David Fryatt, the team's goalkeeper, got to his feet. On behalf of the boys his short, quite amusing speech ended when he told the gathered ensemble that Pat, my wife who often washed the team's kit was, "and finally thanks to Pat, Frank's wife, the team think she's the best scrubber in Essex." I rounded off what was a very enjoyable, and in every respect successful evening. When asked if they would come again next year, 401 hands - including the head waiters - shot heavenward.

In no time at all Easter was upon us. Langton's team, parents, relatives, and friends were seated, comfortably upon the aircraft, anxiously awaiting take-off. All forty-seven of us bound for Blanes, Spain. Three days of sun, sea, sand and tapas. Thanks to a bunch of lads who love to play soccer. The flight was smooth and uneventful. The young Langton team's behaviour impeccable. And so said all four air hostesses who, prior to take off, thought seventeen young boys on board equalled pandemonium. Had they crewed the Scottish flight that landed immediately after us, they might well have been right.

Chapter Seven

All of the Langton party stood gathered on the tarmac, waiting to move inside for passport scrutiny and baggage retrieval. Whilst we did so, the other aircraft slowly taxied and stopped in the passenger disembarkation area. As the stairs were rolled into place, three police cars and a large, windows barred Transit type van, screeched to a halt a short distance away. We were intrigued until the first passenger appeared. As he waved to us, the police and airport personnel moved forward. He descended the first half dozen steps, let go of the stair rail to wave again and fell the rest of the way. Very soon, the stairs at both ends of the fuselage were crowded with heaving, cheering, waving, shouting, singing, staggering, and falling very drunken Scots. In all there were 158 of them, most on the wrong side of sobriety. How many were hurt in falling I never did discover. I could only surmise there were injuries. Furthermore, I hoped none of the fallen were seriously hurt. There had been two Scottish soccer teams on board this special Glasgow football flight. Foolishly, they had congregated in a Scottish pub close to the airport. As they had when they toured in Europe for a good many years. And this year the lucky country chosen was Spain. Langton players thought the whole situation hilarious as it unrolled before them. We told them not to get any ideas. Now I'm wondering, did they? As you will see later. The coach taking us to the Blanes hotel was waiting as our group cleared the airport.

Blanes being slightly less than medium sized, the trip to the hotel was short. Just long enough for me to impress upon my players they were young ambassadors for their country. Also, the beautiful game. Yes, treat our three-day excursion as a short holiday in the sun. Both the people, the language, the food, and football would at first seem strange. Accept that, be on your best behaviour. Impress me, your parents, and those Spanish people you meet, especially those working in the hotel. Do so please and I promise more overseas tours will follow. If you win both games tomorrow and Sunday. Happy Easter. Then came the questions from the team. Most of which were intended to put me on the spot. "Is the ball the same size and shape?" "Does the ref speak English or do we have to question his decisions in Spanish?" "What is boo in Spanish?" "Is bollocks Spanish for bollocks?" (this from fourteen-year olds needed to be, and was reprimanded) Their multi-voiced, jocular reply... "Bollocks." "Can we pretend there is no offside in British football?" I was most relieved when we arrived at our destination.

At first glance, the hotel of Peter's choice was adequately suited to our requirements. Built in the 30's, it was rural, compact and fifty percent occupied by our party. Just a few hundred yards from the beach. The boys' parents and relatives were well pleased with room costs allocated. As indeed they were when told successful fund raising enabled the club to pay their airfares. There was also an excellent 'tapas' bar, which most of our party decided would provide their evening meal. It was only the few who had previously holidayed in Spain, who decided to look for their supper downtown. Peter, I, and our ladies decided the Tapas menu looked enticing, as did many of the others. By eight o'clock, we were the biggest single party gorging Tapas like it was going out of fashion. Because our first game kick off was two o'clock tomorrow, I asked the players' parents not to let the team drink anything intoxicating. And to ensure they went to bed at nine o'clock. God bless them, they did so. Each and every one.

By ten o'clock, our overindulgent, wine fuelled party was in full swing. And in grand voice, especially me, fully throated. It is no boast, but I just love to sing, blessed with a memory enabling me to store the words of the multitude of songs I liked, in my head. So, I led the Langtons' mixed male and female choir. Once underway other English guests carried their chairs to where we were assembled, plonked them as close to us as they could and just let go. The bartenders and waiters already had. The Spanish in the bar who knew some of the songs, joined in. Those who didn't sat and listened. Or left muttering, " The anglaise are crazy." At midnight it was over. Leaving a party of fun loving, song singing, wine guzzling inebriated Brits happy, exhausted and bed bound. And I can honestly say, it was an evening never equalled in my eighty-seven years of life.

The next morning it was the major topic of breakfast conversation, and rightly so. The boys wished they had been present throughout the evening, having been in at the beginning. However, they accepted they were here to play, and win, both games today and tomorrow. Soon the conversation moved onto the teams we were playing. Today's match was a top of the table clash, both teams having finished league champions. In games played hundreds of miles apart. Peter and I were somewhat concerned the pitch was practically grass less. Making it increasingly difficult to read the bounce of the ball. Also, the referee was Spanish and spoke hardly any English. In our pre-match pitch inspection, we both agreed a short passing game would be preferable. Jonesy agreed, not wanting to chase balls to both wings and down the middle in the oppressive heat. It worked a treat, with a 3-1 win in Langton's favour.

Since dropping anchor at the hotel, the players wasted no time in offering the hand of friendship to the staff. Especially the waiters. When we returned to the hotel from our first game, they asked and were told. We won 3-1. They burst into spontaneous cheering and the boys loved it. It was a mutual friendship growing by the hour. We knew very little about our second game opponents. Only that they played in a league one year higher than ours. Consequently, they were playing Under 15 football. When told this, I gave the squad the option of a three-day two game tour, or a two-day one game trip. Their choice was unanimous, accompanied by the confident statement, "And we'll win both." So once again, with the parents' co-operation, our pre-match routine was re-enacted. The boys to their rooms by nine o'clock, lights out by ten. Earlier that day, the hotel manager revealed his brother managed a very good night club, less than half a mile along the beach. It opened at ten o'clock and closed at two a.m. If we wanted to go, he'd ring to arrange it. As last night had been so totally wonderful, we had full house agreement.

Once the boys had gone to their rooms and all was quiet, we set off for the club. We could hear the music, singing and general merriment halfway along the beach. As one, our pace quickened as the party mood once more came upon us. Upon arrival, we Brits were given a rousing welcome. There could be no doubt the hotel manager had phoned his brother to say we were on our way. Once again, we were the largest single party present. In no time at all, we injected what had apparently been missing. That much needed joie de vivre only the Brits can inject when in an atmosphere more suited to a wake. We left, saying our fond farewells

It All Kicks Off On Sunday

to a prolonged ovation. Just as the clock struck 2am. We sang our way all along the beach to the hotel. Only the night porter was there to greet us. I left the main party to escort my wife to our room. Before I left to resume touring the corridors to ensure all was well with the boys, I said, "Let's pretend we are on honeymoon." With no foreign noises emanating from any of the rooms, I doubled my way back to our room. Having enjoyed yet another Brit inspired evening. Watched my wife sink seven Spanish reds. Thoughts of English hanky panky in a Spanish boudoir were uppermost in my mind. Sending a wakeup call to my faithful todger, I quickened my step, undid my belt as I loosened my tie and expectantly entered our room. I thought I had mistakenly walked onto the set of The Sleeping Princess. There and then Terry the Todger, a fervent disciple of passion for the people, no longer stood proud. Defeated, he resumed his disappointing, not to be disturbed posture. Going back to sleep before his next six-monthly call to action. The thoughts and desires of aroused men do oft times go balls up. Or wished they had. Coupled to which, and I know not why, there was a strange foreboding that all was not right with the world...

Chapter Eight

It was an ominous feeling increasing by degrees as I took my seat at the breakfast table. The first inkling I had that trouble was abroad (forgive the pun) on looking around the room. Not one boy was present. Whereas, yesterday morning, the whole team, were there, together with subs, looking very much as though they were eating, not playing for England. Peter said not to worry, they were probably resting before the big game. But I could not help but worry. A few other Mums and Dads wanted to visit the town market, so Pat and I tagged along. We stayed in town for an early lunch, then headed back to the hotel to join the coach taking us to the game. I was always nervous before any game, no matter the level of importance. But this time my nerves kept telling me something was wrong. The boys were unusually quiet. Peter said it was because we were playing an older, bigger team. Probably the hardest and most difficult game they will have ever played since the team was first formed. That helped quell my anxiety. But I could not help feeling something was seriously wrong. There was. The whole bloody team were hung over.

When we finally arrived at the opposition ground, we were greeted by their team of officials. The shaking of hands for Peter and myself took place while the team were escorted to the dressing room. Then their team were lined up for our inspection. That's when my growing sense of alarm went into free fall. They were indeed, overall, the biggest side we had ever met. Each handshake had a firm adult grip. Some of the players were taller than Peter and I. And there was no way, had they tried, to hide the seven o'clock shadows amongst them. The stubble was the giveaway. I would guess this team were a mix of 15-17-year-olds, cobbled together just for our game. And any others arranged by the UK source. In our case it happened to be individuals with Gidea Park, whom we knew well. In my head I was already composing a strong reprimand. Plus, a request for financial reimbursement for the game we played but didn't stand the slightest chance of winning.

They were big, physical, clumsy but fast. We were small, intimidated, trying not to get hurt and slow by comparison. When allowed, we played the better football. Stopped by brute force once inside their eighteen-yard box. We lost 3-0 and spent the return hotel journey in silence. The bigger of our boys counting the bruises. Collected when they tried to match the opposition's physicality. Never had I or Peter experienced such silence when returning from UK away games, most of which as winners. I was concerned as to why, to a boy, they appeared hungover. Without any boy admitting they were, none of them headed the ball. Normally when they could, they did. Especially Peter's son, Steven. When, during the game, I watched him rise high for the ball, then withdraw his head when it arrived, I knew I was right. On arrival at the hotel, as they disembarked from the coach, I herded boys only into the bar. Once seated, I called the head waiter and the bartender to sit with us.

In the past, I very rarely had reason to admonish the team. When Peter or I did, the boys knew it was serious. Or they were in trouble. There were lots of anxious faces. For what seemed an eternity, I built an atmosphere by just sitting and staring at them. Then I began, "What was the last thing I asked all of you before we went out last night?" This met with a wall of silence, so I tried a different approach. "Peter and I are not angry about the match. In truth it was a mismatch which shouldn't have happened. It won't again, because if you don't tell me the truth about how you got the booze last night, there will be no more tours abroad. I've asked the waiters did they take it up to your rooms and they said they didn't. I've asked the barmen did they serve you at the bar and they said no. So, if anybody isn't telling me the truth it must be you. All of you." Suddenly, our goal scoring centre forward got to his feet. I've always encouraged them to treat me as a friend. Tell it as it is. Colin always has.

His opening remarks were delivered with honesty and sincerity I could not refute. "Frank. I speak for all the boys. None of us have lied to you. If you would like to come to the far end of the bar, you will see why not one of us ignored your request." Intrigued, I did as he asked. You will remember earlier, when I described the hotel to you, I said it was built in the 1930's. When the bar was installed a 'dummy waiter' was included for carrying the requirements of the above floors to their required destination. Knowing I said you we're not to go downstairs to order drinks from the bar, you didn't. Armand, a very special friend of the boys, told them of its existence. All they had to do was call the dummy waiter upstairs, place the money and number of pints of cider required on it. Then telephone Armand who told the bar staff to execute the order. It arrived on the first floor with not a drop spilt. Not one of the team went downstairs after the nine o'clock curfew. Not one of the boys went to the bar to order their cider. Not one of the bar staff served any of the boys at the bar. What other could I do except apologise profusely? Colin asked that I did so on bended knee. I did. Together with a pint of cider for each player. A liquid penance. They were also told what I had said about no further tours were now countermanded. But future foreign hotels would not have dummy waiters.

It All Kicks Off On Sunday

Our return flight to the UK was early evening, so the whole party was told they were free to do whatever they pleased. But be back at the hotel sharp at four o'clock. As we were rarely treated to warm sunshine and cloudless skies back home, most of us made for the beach. It was close enough to the beach to either go and get our drinks and eats. There was also a seafood cafe which we kept busy. How the word spread I know not but spread it did. Not immediately, although people drifted in two's and three's to where us Langtonians were enjoying our day in the sun. I was peacefully dozing in the sun, dreaming I could hear Accordion music growing louder and louder. Then a Ukele joined in, plus base guitar. Now voices, both English and Spanish, with a harsh, guttural snatch of German joining in. I awoke with a start. It was lunch time, and I had my own band and chorus. It was the musical magic of Blanes. All around me, a truly European chorus. I was about to join in. What a marvellous finale to be part of before taking our leave of Spain!

There were no further mishaps before the coach deposited, complete, Langton Royals players and supporters at the airport. Vowing to return before the team disbanded. Sadly, we never did, exchanging Blanes for Port Talbot in Wales. Why? Because a family member of John Jones was very involved with a Welsh boys' football club of the same age. Added to which, their parents were willing to put our parents up for the weekend. Expediency and economy preventing yet another fund-raising series of events. Our return from Blanes was almost uneventful. Except when Colin Beaney smuggled his full air sickbag off the aircraft and through customs. The first any passenger on the homeward coach journey knew it too was on board, was when it smacked Jonesy's back of the head. A loud guffaw of laughter greeted the flying missile which then struck Frank Tobin. He was sitting next to his dad who quickly re-launched the still warm sick bag. This time it hit Mrs Cochrane, who screamed loudly. Now the coach driver was aware of the missile and its unacceptable contents. He swiftly braked the coach into the next layby, refusing to move until the culprit reclaimed the offensive sickbag. A very sheepish Beaney took possession of it, until our destination was reached.

Chapter Nine

From a very young age, I enjoyed listening to music. Added to which I developed a pleasant voice. I occasionally considered taking voice training lessons. Had I done so successfully, my life might well have followed a totally different direction. I can imagine being introduced as the singing referee. It wasn't until my mid-forties, and purely by chance, a client heard me singing quietly to myself in his reception. His name was David Baker, and he was the company's managing director. He was my client and had been for the best part of four years. Yet not once did he ever let on that he was a long-standing member of South Woodham Ferrers Male Voice Choir.

I did not hear him coming down the stairs to collect me. Only a voice saying, "Frank, we've got room for you in our choir." I always thought I could sing a bit. Not a lot but enough to hold my own when asked. Now here I was. Being asked by the MD of my second largest client. I could hardly refuse. I was in my early forties when I first gazed upon my fellow choristers. All 60 plus men who looked old enough to have to have crewed the maiden voyage of HMS Pinafore. They were virtually the closest thing I've ever seen to a Geriatric Glee Club.

It didn't interfere with managing Langton Royals. Or my Sunday youth football refereeing. In fact, it proved to be an unexpected bonus in fund raising events, by way of arranging annual concerts for the club. Now a member of a four-part male voice choir. A very nervous first base (baritone). Learning the art of mime as I was expected to quickly learn the lyrics of all 103 pieces in the choir's repertoire. Never once did we appear on stage with music in hand. That was taboo. So, you learned the words or honed the art of mime to perfection.

Before I joined, I imagined a MVC to be any number of blokes getting together to sing songs they enjoyed. Four-part harmonies, dynamics, crescendos and the likes were unchartered waters. My beliefs were simple. Ignore the others, sing your heart out. Then stardom would or could be mine. I would or could be a celebrity. Sadly, fame and fortune never came calling. It was an apprenticeship I served mainly because of one word - "afterglow". A magical happening which followed each concert. That is, provided there was a Pub within elbow lifting arm's length distance. We just loved it. To stand, pint in hand, singing and enjoying the moment. We did. Then so did the drinking public. Provided it was songs they knew, which we made certain they did.

Looking back on the years spent as a chorister under SWFMVC Music Director Stephen Rumsey, I enjoyed every minute while becoming a seasoned songster. It continued throughout my time with this established choir. Especially when an idea I had for recruiting new members might well have hit the singing jackpot. I did not remain with SWFMVC long enough to give it a whirl.

For reasons never explained, nor understood, the main body of the choir were told that our much-appreciated Music Director was leaving. As it transpired, it was not his decision, but the committee's. Almost without exception, the rest of us were disappointed. Especially when we were told the name of Stephen's replacement. I had been a happy South Woodham Ferrers chorister for over 15 years. After just one month I was no more. Living in Galleywood, I made enquiries about Chelmsford's resident choir. They invited me to join them at their next rehearsal. I did and became their forty seventh member. A baritone doubling second tenor. The first concert they gave was on 26th November 1903 in Chelmsford's Old Corn Exchange. Raising funds for Essex Chronicle's Boer War Fund. Ticket price three shillings. If any gentleman reading this is contemplating joining a choir, let me explain who a male voice choir is for. Put quite simply, MEN.

Who have wondered what it is like to sing in a choir.

Who think they can't sing and are willing to receive a pleasant surprise.

Who want a creative group activity.

Who did sing once but haven't for a long time.

Who sing elsewhere but are looking to broaden their experience.

Who are constantly sought by MVC's, nationally.

Chapter Ten

Langton Royals were sitting comfortably on top of the under 15 Belhus and District League. So far, we had won all games bar one and were league leaders. The draw was against the team lying third, when four of our first team players were laid low with a strain of Asian flu. This was the game whose home supporters were true to form in their continual use of loud and bad language. And so they did today. It was one of those Sundays when Richard's mother, Edna, decided to watch him play. Across the park were the home side's supporters, among whom was the profanity queen of East Ham. Hair in curlers and turbaned, stained apron that had long seen better days, rolled down stockings, a hand rolled cigarette only removed from her mouth to make way for the next wave of profane rhetoric. Edna was shocked by the continual outbursts directed at her son together with the rest of Langton players. Unable to contain herself any longer, Edna took matters into her own hands. She shouted across the park, "Oi You!" "Who me?" returned the turban. "Yes you," cried Edna. "When I say shit... jump on the shovel." Both sets of supporters fell about, as turban head swiftly returned to the dressing room, head bowed never to return. I thanked Edna profusely for ridding football of one of its unwanted crass supporters.

We expected to complete the league and cup back-to-back double. Though we were comfortable league champions, complacency robbed us of the cup. Our opponents finished in the lower league positions. Fifth from bottom if I remember correctly. Try as Pete and I did to warn the team it wasn't just a question of turning up and the cup was ours. On the day, the opposition played out of their skin. We finally woke up with just minutes left to play. The score was 2 - 2 and they fought for every ball. It paid off, when, from a corner in the dying seconds, they slotted home the winner. For them the cup. For us. Beaten finalists' medals. No less than our complacency deserved.

I faced the coming under 16 league fixtures with misgivings. Months before the start I told Peter that I wanted him to take over the team management. It would then give me the opportunity to concentrate on refereeing youth games played in East Anglia at weekends. Also, weekdays if weather conditions led to weekend cancellations. He was happy to oblige, but with some reservation. Long before the season ended, many of the team would be seventeen. Their hormones dictated that beautiful girls were likely to take preference over the beautiful game. We knew the problems this would create. Late Saturday nights would be partnered by late Sunday morning wakeups and missed kick offs. Plus, an assortment of hangovers demanding stay in bed cures. Also, how senior teams would poach our better team players. This was not purely conjecture. It happens to the best of teams. So be it with Langton's who finished the under sixteen season mid-table. It was a problem season for Peter, no thanks to the pitfalls mentioned earlier. I had written to all the team players and parents. Pointing out that Peter would be manager for the coming season. Allowing me to undertake a full season refereeing youth football fixtures throughout East Anglia. Had I remained manager for this, the last season before we took our final bow, it would have remained the same. Langton Royals never kicked another ball in league competition.

Chapter Eleven

There is a long-established London Welsh MVC who gather other male choirs to sing with them at The Albert Hall. This is a two-yearly concert date, wherein a thousand voices join. The London Welsh chooses who the guest choirs will be. Taking this as a measure of competence, to be invited twice, demonstrates how highly you are rated by the London Welsh MVC. We were selected in 2014 and 2016. Sadly, due to serious financial business difficulties, I was forced to sell the house and to leave Galleywood. So, I missed both, but not before I tried the idea mentioned earlier.

Male choirs are forever keen to expand their number of choristers. Chelmsford was no exception. I told the committee what I had in mind. They gave me the go ahead. I wrote a five-page laid back introduction to who, what and why choirs exist. Then had every choir member deliver two hundred copies to 200 neighbours either side of their address. The mailing ended with an invitation to attend a rehearsal to look, learn and listen. Accompanied by wives if they so desired. In normal circumstance, choirs are lucky to recruit 3-5 members. This night they never stopped coming, and we hit the jackpot. 28 men, quite a few with wives attended, stayed and listened. 23 signed on the dotted line. That night we grew our membership from 48 to 72. I was the man of the moment.

Sadly, I had no option other than to sell our Galleywood home and move to Suffolk. The new journey made it impossible for me to remain a Chelmsford chorister. I left just as the Albert Hall request arrived. The choir I loved were invited to join the London Welsh choir. Not once but twice. To this day it remains the saddest goodbye and bitterest regret of all time. And still is!

Being fit and no longer tied to any youth football team, my referee credentials stood me in good stead. Sunday was normally my favourite fixture. I was registered with the two strongest leagues in Barking/Dagenham and Romford/Hornchurch youth football. I looked upon my pseudonym of Red Frank as a campaign medal. Worn with pride. I was as happy to oblige the Under 10's as I was the Under 16's. With the very young, it was rare to find fouls were committed with intent. Usually, it was because of timing or rules of the game, of which they lacked understanding. I nevertheless penalised the player and explained the reason why. I got as much out of coaching the young players as I did out of refereeing their games. I've been praised by dads for "not letting them get away with it" which I appreciated. I've also been clouted with both a handbag and umbrella for "picking on my son" and "you 're a bloody bully, he's only a baby." On both occasions I asked the team manager to have a word with them. Then neither incident would be included in my 'It all kicks off on Sunday' report.

Oh that I could say the same about teenaged and adult football. On too many occasions I wished I had the power to remove all supporters from the side-lines. Or make them read and understand the rules of the game, before being allowed to watch the match. Better still, make all club appointed linesmen sit and pass exams as they affected the job, they are there to do. Then report supporter incidents that interfered with them during the game. These to be included in the referee's report.

Like so many referees I have met during the years I've been the man in the middle, tales to tell are manifest. Apart from insults, criticisms and threats, I've been sworn at, spat at, and kicked by retards posing as supporters. Items thrown at me or onto the pitch during matches include coins, empty drink cans and plastic bottles, rotting fruit. Even human and animal excrement left on the bonnet or smeared on the windscreen of my car. All four tyres deflated. Often enough for me to carry a foot pump in the boot. I knew when I would call it a day. And I decided to write and submit full reports to the League referee's secretary whenever the more serious of the above incidents took place. I wanted the guilty clubs responsible, seriously reprimanded, heavily fined, kicked out of the league. Then report them to the FA in order they would be blacklisted by all local football leagues in Essex.

In the final two years of officiating, I informed each club manager whose supporters committed any of the offences listed, they would be reported to the league secretary. Those concerned, gave me their promise to treat the incidents I reported, seriously. And they did. The sixteen-year-old who left me flat on my back was banned sine die. Which meant at sixteen years of age he was barred from ever playing competitive league football again.

At the age of seventy-two I decided enough was enough. No dramatic farewells. I blew the whistle for the last time. Ending the last game, I would ever referee. Collected my hard-earned fee of £15.00. Shook the hand of both managers. Walked away from the pitch and just kept on walking. There would be no more Sunday animosity. No longer would I need to defend my decisions at tribunals or appeals. No more angry confrontations. No more accusations that I was fatherless. No more threats addressed to me and members of my family. No more attempts to keep the peace amongst twenty-two so called sportsmen. Intent on causing serious damage to each other in the name of football. Amateur or professional. No more dodging angry handbag or umbrella swinging players' mothers. From that moment forth I exchanged the ever-present dangers of the beautiful Sunday game for a leisurely stroll and beautiful Sunday pint or two.

Looking back over the many years I have been actively involved in and with football, the game has changed beyond recognition. For the princely sum of three pence old money, I was privileged to enjoy an exciting Saturday whenever Charlton played at home. The first game I watched was at the age of eight. It was 1942 and Charlton were playing Portsmouth. They brought enough supporters with them to completely fill the North Stand. It was the first time I ever heard massed voice singing at a football match. Even though Portsmouth lost, they never stopped singing the "Pompey Chimes". I believe it is still sung today. Eighty years on, I also believe it's now expected that all professional football clubs' supporters sing. The difference being unlike Portsmouth, the antagonistic verses now sung are full of hateful lyrics and disgusting profanities. Yes, I am 87 years old. Sadly, I've had to sit and watch our national sport fall foul of untold money. Ask any soccer fan to name the clubs who, season after season, will fill the top five positions in the Premier league. Then ask them why. If they are honest, they will give you a one single word answer. MONEY!

The second world war was nearing its end. I was taken by uncle Cyril and my cousin Derek to watch Charlton versus Fulham. It was the very first time I had watched a London derby. I loved what I saw and became a lifetime supporter of Charlton Athletic. They won 3-1 and from then on, to the present day, I was/am a lifetime supporter. I was over the moon when they reached the 1946 Cup Final. It was a hard-fought game with all the goals coming in extra time. Derby County finished the stronger, winning 4-1. I was twelve years old and heartbroken. Unbelievably, Charlton reached the cup final again the following year. This time their opponents were Burnley. Once again, I watched this cup final from "Winkle" Taylor's house. They were one of the very few families who then owned a television. It was a tough end-to-end game, with Charlton winning 1-0. Tiny left winger Chris Duffy scored the only goal. Ran the full length of the pitch before leaping into the arms of full back Shreeve. Through thick and thin they've been my team. Sadly, although occasionally flattering to deceive, my eighty years of loyal support have been rewarded by sweet FA (forgive the pun).

Chapter Twelve

In the same eighty years, football has changed beyond recognition. From club owners, chairman, managers, stadiums, laws of the game, players and their earnings, foreign players per club, transfer fees and team supporters. I could include seating instead of standing on terraces. But it would seem this is an area of change soon to revert to standing. I understand the supporters prefer it as it was. Personally, I believe one very good reason is the ability to hurl objects farther when standing. And standing, whatever it is to be thrown, especially coinage, has a better chance of striking a moving object. This I've witnessed on too many occasions.

As you no doubt know, octogenarians prefer to look back. Understandable when at 87, one assumes there's precious little lying ahead to look forward to. In doing so, I believe the only things remaining unchanged from football of the fifties to present day are the pitch markings, the goal posts, nets, and corner flags. But changes to the game itself and many of its corresponding laws, mean for me it is no longer the beautiful game. Now my preferred sport is Rugby Union. Why? I believe when, in 1961 the capped wages of £20.00 weekly for professional soccer players were scrapped. That's when it started. Immediately one player made the headlines. His name, Johnny Haynes of Fulham, and England. His weekly club earnings jumped from twenty pounds to one hundred pounds, weekly. Then there was the lifting of ruling that all clubs were allowed to sign one foreign player. This then became three players each until this was also ditched. Now it is just as many as you like and can afford. I wondered how far away the team is where every footballer on the park is a foreign player. Probably before I'm playing for a celestial eleven on cloud seven. Should it happen, would they have the balls to call the team English. Believe it or not, since then it happened to Chelsea in January 2022. Every player they had playing on the park that day was indeed foreign.

I curse the day when footballing's gang of wealthy club owners sanctioned the Premier division. The game I had known all my life was no more. Having lifted the £20.00 capped wages agreement, six figure plus weekly wages paid now are not unusual. Not only for the privileged few, mainly imported foreign premier top echelon players. But all those playing with the top five premier clubs. So wealthy you can name the clubs who will finish in the premier top five. Season after season. Today, each player has an Agent who, when representing his client's best interests, adds millions to the cost demanded before the transfer negotiations are completed.

When I qualified as a referee, I was swearing allegiance to upholding the existing laws of the game. They were religiously applied no matter the age level of the teams concerned. It saddens me that today's officials are being advised to "let the game flow". In England's world qualifying games against Italy, Denmark, Croatia and Hungary, all four referees certainly did. Sticking to the strict laws of the game, I would have sent at least four players off for a mix of violent conduct, dangerous play, and dissent. As it was, they were either shown a yellow card or vocally reprimanded. I was further angered by the profane language and racial chants both sets of fans were guilty of. Continuously and

It All Kicks Off On Sunday

throughout most of the matches. It's boring. As are the long spells of possession football played by England, the ball being short passed in their own half. As exciting as a game of championship chess.

All too often my mind reverts to the attacking game played throughout the fifties/sixties (remember 1966?) and seventies. A fan as loyal to Charlton, then in the old first division, as I am today. Arsenal visiting the Valley. Ground packed solid, (a rumoured 72,000). Watching players arriving by tram. Boots carried in brown paper bags. Children passed over the heads of mixed fans to the very front of the crowds. Vision now perfect. Both teams playing attacking football from the first whistle. A game full of goals. Charlton winning 5-4 thanks to a Charlie Vaughan hat trick. Two of his three goals by headers. Sam Bartram's super saves for Charlton, in the dying seconds. Ninety minutes of exciting end-to-end soccer. Shaking hands all round by players, managers, supporters. Players signing autographs long after the final whistle. Cycling home, each of the nine goals scored, indelibly imprinted on your mind. That is the beautiful game which, sadly, will never be seen again. Bring it back and my growing enjoyment of Rugby Union would be put on hold.

There is no distance in time, only memories. At age 87, I have plenty of them. I would like to say that many were shared with my dad. Sadly, not possible as he died aged 24. l was only four months old and my sister four years. Leaving my mum, a very young widow with two very young children. I have never stopped wondering how different my life could have been with a dad's involvement in my career path. Although out of necessity, my mother remarried. I believe I was three when she did. Not old enough to have been asked an opinion. A pity because it was a sad, bad marriage. We moved into my new stepfather's very small house in Creek Road, Deptford. A virtual slum. It was the second marriage for both. Both had children. Fortunately, only one of his children was of an age to still be living at home. Even so, there was little or no room with only two bedrooms.

The second world war was just beginning when we were given a council house in Kidbrooke. This was a very large re-housing development in Southeast London. History will tell you although Chamberlain, our Prime Minister, had declared war when Adolph Hitler, ordered his armies to invade Poland, it was declared a phoney war, inactive for six months. In truth, despite a war of words, Hitler was busily developing his armies, weapons, but most of all aircraft. Chamberlain and his government were lulled into believing the phoney war could and would be settled by negotiation. Whilst we kept talking, he kept increasing his armament and military strength. Without warning, he launched his invasion of Poland. So began the invasion of Europe. The real war had begun, and we were caught napping.

Readers of my first book published earlier this year will know how the war affected my family. For me it was an adventure, until we were lucky to have survived the loss of our house. It then became a reality. The final defeat of Hitler and his henchmen was a long time coming. The loss of life unacceptable. We survived, but my mother suffered at the hands of my stepfather. He was a wife beater who spent most of the war propping up the bar of the local pub, the Dover Patrol. Usually, drunk when he arrived home, he would pick on my mother in front of my sister and I. Mum's friends and neighbours virtually begged her to leave him. Because of us she wouldn't. As I grew older and into my teens, I told him, hit her again and I would forcibly stop him. His brutalising ceased soon after the war ended. But the damage had been done and she died of a stroke in her

50's. Once again, I had been deprived of a father's guiding hand throughout my early working years.

I was married when she died. She idolised both of my sons and had the pleasure of nursing my daughter for six weeks. It was totally unexpected. I was a delegate at a conference when she was found collapsed. I was asked to leave the seated audience and go to the organising office. There I was told it was my father who had died. How anybody could make such a mistake I never did discover. It was a shattering shock for me. Even more so for my sister who, thanks to my stepfather's earlier wartime behaviour, grew to hate him with a vengeance. It proved to be the end of my Kidbrooke family. Both Gwen, my sister, and I were married and had long since departed the family home. For the second time, as it was destroyed during a wartime air aid. Now, only Mick, my stepbrother, Gwen and I, mum and Arthur Luff, stepfather were living at the Kidbrooke address. Unbeknown to me or Gwen, Mick had impregnated a young neighbourhood girl. Name of Jean. He now had a son and without any warning he suddenly and silently departed with both, plus his father. In time I discovered they were living In Cornwall. However, Gwen and I had no wish to contact him. The last chapter of this unhappy family saga remains unwritten. And will stay that way.

Chapter Thirteen

From the moment I was no longer actively involved in football, I channelled my interests and energies into helping rescue and rehome small animals. Both Pat, Nic, my daughter, and both granddaughters were already physically helping SeSaw. A local small animal rescue and rehoming charity. Maggie and her husband opened the rescue centre in the late 1900's. He died four years ago, leaving Maggie and her band of volunteers to battle on. Nobody could possibly have foreseen the advent of the Covid 19 virus. Nor the length of time it would remain with us. Or the havoc it would reap.

Like most small charities, within a year many were financially desperate. Having no idea how long the pandemic would prevent their successfully proven fund-raising events from being reinstated. It's then it struck me. Here Today "GOON" Tomorrow. The book I had long considered writing, could now become a reality. With monies raised, given to Sesaw. It proved my belief that Octogenarians prefer to live in the past. Able to make comparisons with the then and now. From infancy to my senior years, the memories came crowding in. Many and often. From start to finish I wrote Here Today 'GOON' Tomorrow in ten weeks. What now? I asked myself, realising the period of my life covered was only from birth to National Service in the Royal Air Force. I did not want to leave it there. Once more I applied the octogenarian rule of thumb. Encouraged by those who had enjoyed reading "GOON" I once more realised there was a second book, Well Worth Waiting For, potentially resting in the wings. I never held back and in a slightly longer passage of time, my second book was published in October. Revealing the many numerous and often humorous memoirs. Occurring during my first senior employment to present day. Whether or not I am an author I ask you to be the judge. But once again it was well received. Now, before I say farewell, I believe "It All Kicks Off on Sunday" will be my last book.

It recalls my time spent as a boys' football club manager and coach. Plus, my forty plus years as a qualified football referee. It recounts battles I had with young and adult players. But more especially, parents and club supporters. Will it be the last? At this moment in time, I believe the answer to be yes. As with the previous two books, royalties realised by sales will include £5.00 donated to SeSaw for each book sold locally. By buying my books, both SeSaw and I sincerely thank you for helping us help those unable to help themselves. Finally, a question. Have you seen the large number of blue discs appearing on dog collars recently.

An idea of Battersea dog and cats' home, they represent the wearer is a genuine rescued dog/cat. Recently introduced, it's growing in leaps and bounds and already estimated to be eight and a half million in Great Britain. Strongly endorsing my long held, unshakeable beliief. We are the biggest nation of kind, active and enduring dog lovers. To be found anywhere in the world. It's a great idea, and all sixteen members of my family are proud to be lifetime members. Why not join us?

Chapter Fourteen

Throughout our sixty-three years of married life, every member of our sixteen-strong family have together developed a great love of all animals. Both large and small. It began when Pat, my wife had, as a small child, a maiden aunt name of Beryl. She was a member of the Zoological Society. One of the privileges of membership was being able to visit London Zoo. Usually early on selected Sundays. Before the general public were allowed in. As a treat she would take Pat. Can you imagine how a young girl enjoyed being allowed to feed dog biscuits to Giraffes in their enclosure? Taking Penguins for a walk. Hold while hand feeding all manner of small animals, until she and Beryl departed for home. A youngster's dream come true. It's where her all-embracing animal fondness began, never to disappear. It has governed my married life, together with that of the whole family. Strongly expressed by the number of dogs rescued by Pat and me - fifteen to date. Add those rescued by other family members and the total is twenty-two. All stayed with us. For the remainder of their canine lives.

While I was travelling on business in the UK and Europe. Immersed in matters football at home, we bought a four-bedroom house at Galleywood. A suburb of Chelmsford. Not only was it a delightful property, but it also satisfied the final of Pat's desires. It stood in two acres of land. Apart from the dogs - by now we had five living with us in a four-bedroom house. We also had two ponies stabled in two horse boxes on land at the back. Fonzie was just 11.2 hands, bought for Nic to ride at gymkhanas. It wasn't long before she had outgrown him. She agreed to let Fonzie go when she had a bigger horse. It wasn't long before we found Flame. At 14.2 hands he fitted her size and my pocket. By now, Fonzie had become a family favourite. When I said he had to go, I was besieged and deluged by the tears of Nic and her horsey pals. So, I had no option other than to let him stay. It meant building stables and fencing our land. To which of course I had to agree. By this time, Pat's father had died and Sylvia, her mother, was living with us.

Whether it was planned, intentional or simply coincidental, animals of varied description, size and breed must have heard we were a soft touch. The first and largest was to greet me when I went to pay my respect to Pat's first rescue. As I went through the garden gate, there they were. Large as life and twice as ugly. Two of the fiercest Pot-Bellied Pigs you ever did see. I don't know who was most surprised. Them or me. But I do know who ran the fastest and farthest. Me. It was the beginning of A Noah's Ark two by two passenger style recruitment. Sheep, goats, ducks, chickens and now three horses Why three? Nick had a friend of 18 who became pregnant. She could no longer afford to pay for her horse's stabling. Could we stable Solitaire, her horse, until after the baby was born? Yes, said Nic. It was the longest pregnancy ever. Solitaire was still with us fourteen years later.

April 21, 2022, Her Majesty Queen Elizabeth 11 was ninety-six. I was 88. We've both led very busy lives. At very different levels of course. Ask the first Corgi you happen upon what is it we both had in common. You will get a two-word answer. Dogs and horses. It would seem we both have had lots of each in our lifetimes. Certainly, true for Pat and

I where dogs were a prime concern. At one time we had no less than five living with us. They included a Parsons Jack Russell and an Irish Wolf Hound. All rescued, having been abandoned, brutalised mostly abroad or whose owners had died. I talk more about this a little further on.

Early on, I mentioned as well as Football, I was also actively involved in playing golf and angling. The former less and less when I finally registered a handicap of fourteen. Then playing time needed to reduce my handicap further just wasn't available. Not so Angling, whenever an opportunity presented itself. Both freshwater-at least once a weekend in the Spring to Autumn. Sea fishing once monthly on a weekend all year round. I was latterly, a member of two clubs and skipper of the sea fishing club. My main function was to organise which coastal ports we sailed from. We favoured South and East coast trips wherein because of the known shallow depths of water, no matter the tide, we all adopted up tide casting. The skipper would set the boat for the mark he decided we were to fish. The eight of us on board would draw for fishing positions. Then we would set up the method and tackle, baiting the hook with each angler's preferred bait. Then sitting patiently, waiting until the skipper reached the chosen mark. On board was equipment, enabling him to search the seabed for fish before deciding X marked the spot. He then dropped anchor. Once she settled, all eight anglers cast their bait as far from the boat as possible. Now the waiting began.

With the serious business now underway, the money stakes came into play. It was universally agreed that apart from catching fish, £2.00 each angler would be won for - the first fish caught; the heaviest fish landed; the heaviest catch of the day, of qualifying fish. Weighed in by the skipper before he upped anchor and headed for home. Before I introduced money into the equation, if bites were slow and few and far in between, it was too easy for the not too serious angler to lose interest. Now, each section winner would receive £14.00. Win all three and you became richer by £42.00. Add to it the money value of the heaviest bag caught and you would have enjoyed one hell of a supreme day's fishing.

From the first year of money being introduced, I was winner twice. On each occasion I ran the risk of being thrown overboard. I made the most of being the best sea angler on board. Until we came ashore. Something nobody except the skipper could dispute. And I loved it. The first time I ever went sea fishing was during two weeks in Cornwall. We went on holiday with Stan, a business friend. We became quite friendly with our landlord, Mervin. He invited the both of us to join him for an afternoon's sea fishing. Apparently, the local trawlermen had spotted a large shoal of fish three miles offshore. He hoped they would stay where seen. He also hoped they were Conger Eels. Fish that were seasonally seen in the area. They were favoured by restaurants, who had someone in the harbour, waiting to buy the fishing parties' conger eel catch.

Once anchored where the large shoals had been reported, Mervin set Stan and I up with hand lines. The favoured way of catching mackerel. His own heavy fishing rig was intended for the Conger. After an hour, whilst we had landed enough mackerel to feed a small army, Mervin hadn't had a single bite. He was contemplating moving to another mark when it happened. "Gotcha, you bastard." Mervin shouted, "Get me the large net on top of the cabin. Whatever it is, it's bloody big." Fifteen minutes later, its head broke water. It wasn't just big. It... was... HUGE. Its tail walked to the stern of the boat, where Stan and I were cowering. Thank God Mervin, large net in hand, steered it back and into the net on his second attempt. Neither of us had ever seen a conger eel before. So, this monster from the deep decided to show us his fighting prowess. Free of the net, he thrashed his way to the stern, where the two of us were clutching each other.

Stan screamed. I got ready to leap overboard, imploring Mervin to "kill the bastard or I'll jump." He couldn't move as he was doubled up with laughter. Having seen he'd frightened Stan and I half to death. And now, much weakened from his fighting in the sea and on the boat, the conger quit scrapping, much to our relief. Long, long after and on the way back to Brighton, we ran into a shoal of conger. The skipper dropped anchor and eight anglers got in amongst them. I was soon fighting a very weighty fish. I finally got its head above water, and it was Cornwall all over again. It was a very large Conger (42lbs)) and there were two others, already being played.

It was the first time we'd been out with this skipper and his new boat. Once he'd dropped anchor he disappeared into his cabin. Only to re-appear to tell us he was going to try another mark closer to shore. Consequently, we kept our tackle intact. Only changing to a fresh bait. It was pure fluke we ran into the shoal of conger. They were heading out to sea as we were heading in shore. Most unusual to have three of the six rods fishing with fish securely hooked. The skipper panicked and left the netting to us. The other two were in single figures, both smaller than mine. They were soon on board. Mine fought to the last and I was exhausted when Alan finally got him on board with the Gaff. He weighed 42 lbs.

I was delighted as people from Brighton's restaurants would be waiting when we landed. The reason is they wanted conger and were paying three pounds per pound for them. I could not believe my luck. Being paid £142 pounds for doing what I absolutely loved. Or rather I would have been. If only the boat proud idiot of a skipper had not insisted on tying my fish to the outside of his precious boat. Why? Because he didn't want a mess on board and my conger was too big to fit into the fish boxes on the boat. Somewhere between there and the harbour, the biggest fish I ever caught was washed away. I would have hit him had Alan not stepped in between us. I suppose it was some sort of consolation as I now held the club conger record. As well as the skate record from a previous sea trip.

Chapter Fifteen

Are you one of those people who, like me, whenever their ship comes in, are too often at the airport? Fortunately, it only happens now and again. But when it does it's all too often costly as well as bitterly disappointing. When it happened in 2008 the loss of potentially high rewards remains with me to the present day. It began when I spotted a small advertisement in the Daily Mail. It was for a Spanish company with Poole, Dorset based subsidiary offices. They required an Essex based main agent to sell prestige villas on the beautiful Costa Blanca coastline.

They wanted applicants prepared to fly to Spain to meet Euro Prestige Villas headquarter staff. They would be taken on a tour of the 30 sites currently being developed along 37 miles of this magnificent coastline. Where the company were building apartments, town houses, penthouses, bungalows and villas. They had been doing so for over 30 years and to date had successfully completed and sold 10,000 homes to British purchasers in the healthiest place in Europe. Where those living enjoy 325 days of warm sunshine each and every year.

Having Pat's agreement to spend a weekend in the sun, I rang the Dorset office. Explaining although over sixty, I was readily available and raring to go. Tom, the UK's managing director quickly put my mind at rest regarding my age. He gave me the dates of the weekend and welcomed me aboard. All that was needed was to send the cost of two low-cost flights and we were heading for sea, sand and guaranteed sun. The flight was uneventful, and Tom was there to personally greet us when we touched down in sunny Spain. During the flight, Pat and I wondered who else were flying for the same purpose as us. There were two. One of either sex and both half our age.

We were taken to the head office and made most welcome by the Spanish staff. It was a relaxed, delightful tapas luncheon accompanied by excellent bottles of local wine. All served on the roof of the company. The totally relaxed atmosphere and gentle way of life filled both Pat and I with envy. As soon as lunch was over, members of Euro Prestige Villas staff launched into a well-rehearsed, informative know your company, its people, history, and product range presentation. Followed by what was expected of the Essex main agent, including what he or she could expect in terms of support from Spain. We were then set free to do as we wished, which included spending the rest of the day on the beach. Or enjoying superb shopping precincts and restaurants downtown, or both. Whatever Pat and I, and the two singles who had travelled with us from the UK, fancied. Tom had arranged to meet us for dinner that evening. At the end of an interesting meal cooked by a Swedish chef, Tom left us. Before he did, he arranged to pick us up at 9am the following morning for a grand tour of some of the 30 sites in various development stages. We walked back to the Hotel, stopping for a nightcap en route. It was soon after midnight when we decided to call it a day.

Tom arrived in the morning and at 9 o'clock we were on our way to view examples of the properties we would be selling. That was provided we were contracted as the Essex main agent. Both of us were gobsmacked by the magnificent standard of build. Also, the interior finish of each of the properties we inspected. Best of all was the extreme care applied to each chosen site's selection. The delightful panoramic vista of each was superb, whichever way you looked. After viewing each type of property on our way to lunch, my comment to Pat was, "I don't know about selling love, if we are appointed, I'll be buying." You just could not fault the product range. Prices were affordable, the pace of life both gentle and relaxed, a believable lack of crime, superb shopping precincts and restaurants, with excellent and inspirationally varied cuisines. Things which regrettably have become increasingly difficult to find and afford in the UK.

Tom drove us to the airport, just 25 minutes from company HQ. I felt both Pat and I had impressed him sufficiently to be considered for the position of Essex main agents. We were both in our mid 60's and could devote the time necessary in building a successful sales platform whilst continuing to service our existing business activities. I had four advertising accounts, the biggest of which was Dictaphone whom I had been serving for the past four years. My contact was an American, Bill Cottle, Managing Director. We worked together very well, and I now had his respect, both socially and in business.

When they launched the hand-held portable pocket-sized Dictation machine, the American based CEO told Bill to use the American created advertising campaign in its entirety. I was aghast. It was totally all American and not at all suitable for the English market. Bill immediately booked two flights and at the weekend, he and I were USA bound. I had three days in which to provide the complete press advertising, marketing, and public relations campaign. Me and my big mouth!

I asked the Shape team to produce finished roughs of the campaign Bill had previous seen, liked and approved. They burned the midnight oil working the roughs into a high standard of presentation finish. Both the advertising campaign and supporting material was absolutely first class. Bill simply loved it and expressed his heartfelt thanks to each of the Shape team concerned. We flew to New York on Sunday. My presentation was to be to Dictaphone's CEO, total American Sales and Marketing personnel. Unbeknown to me, also Dictaphone's American Advertising Agency's Al Paul Lefton's account handling team. Halfway through the presentation, I could see from the gathered audience reaction we were on a winner. Bill led the applause, whilst the CEO's acceptance speech when I had finished, surprisingly agreed I was right. Right to have rejected the American product launch campaign material. He said we were right with our "horses for courses" promotions platform.

Within three months, building a direct selling platform for our Euro Prestige Villa properties on the Costa Brava was, to say the least, pleasing. I had already booked a weekend viewing trip for one of my four Agency clients. I could accompany Scott and his wife but being my first potential buyer, Tom agreed to meet them when they arrived. To me, this was as good as being my first sale. If Tom was as good as I thought his sales ability was, then apparently my income from this one sale could be as high as £10,000. And already we had other contacts showing genuine interest in making the weekend trip soon. Plus, Pat had already selected the villa of our choice. You can imagine the bitter disappointment when we were told everything was put on hold. Apparently, the Spanish head office had expanded their future development programme without counting the cost. They were now looking for financial investment. It wasn't forthcoming, nor was our first pay day. And with the Spanish economy in freefall, we had no alternative but to walk away from Spain and all we believed it would mean concerning our future.

Chapter Sixteen

Helping those who cannot help themselves. It was something I had often thought of doing. But gainfully employed and working full out, I could never find the time. At the age of 87 and with time on my hands, it was now or never. So, I set out to write my first book. I have now completed and published two, with the third well on its way.

The first, Here Today "Goon" Tomorrow, was published in July. The second, Well Worth Waiting For was published in October. Together they chronicle the story of my life. The third, It All Kicks Off on Sunday, is of the years spent as a boys' football team founder, coach and manager. Together with forty plus years as a fully qualified football referee. The story of the countless battles with adult and junior players, their managers, supporters and parents. Hence the title It All Kicks Off on Sunday. Rest assured, it is the voice of experience.

Married in 1958, both my wife and three children share a great love of animals, especially dogs. Rescued dogs. The first on our first-born son's birthday. Today the total is fifteen. Each remaining with us for the whole of their canine lives. If you add to the dogs rescued by others of my family, now sixteen strong, the number to date is twenty-two. Will there be more? At 88 and 84, Pat and I know time is running out. It's unlikely for us. But not the family!

That is why we are giving £5.00 to SeSaw from each and every book sold. They are a small animal rescue and rehoming charity in Leavenheath, Suffolk. They, like all small charities, have suffered severe financial losses due to the Pandemic. But still they battle on. Their needs are far greater than mine. My wife, daughter and grandchildren all physically help with SeSaw's animal welfare. Today book sales have raised more than £2,500, which has been donated to them. Once It All Kicks Off on Sunday is published, I can continue my hobby of collecting 18th and 19th century mugs.

Early on in my first days of mug and jug collecting. Almost exclusively from Antique Fairs and Auctions. I learned of and joined a series of antique evening classes. Not only was I able to expand my knowledge of a much broader range of antiques. It's where I met Ray, who like me, wanted to improve his knowledge of all things ancient and collectible. His specialist knowledge of antique drinking glasses was, like mine, much broadened. So much so, we decided to work as a team and launch our own trading company.

The name registered was R&F Antiques. I first suggested F&R, as it was alphabetical. But no. He insisted it must be the other way round. His knowledge of antique buying and selling was greater than mine. I should have been warned off there and then. He was the most self-centred, selfish, spoilt twenty-two-year-old cussed only child I ever had the misfortune to cross opinions with. He had chosen to live between his parents and partner's homes. He, she, and they continually argued, and I was expected to take sides. He regularly paid too much for re-sale items, especially Royal Worcester porcelain pieces. He also booked stalls in distant antique fairs without ever intending to attend. This left me to build and man our stand. He would then arrive halfway through the day, laden with items he wanted to show.

That is until I discovered most of these items were his, not R&F's. He argued that I had agreed to this. When discussing how our entrance into fairs and table-top events was to be conducted. Typical Ray bullshit!

As far as I was concerned, our partnership ended right there. I told him exactly what I thought of his behaviour in the nine months R&F had traded. I pulled no punches and physically came close to throwing a few. Much to the amusement of other stall holders and gathering visitors. I told him that as I had been there since early morning. And as he had just arrived, I was leaving him to look after the stand, break it down when the show ended. Removing my items, I left for home, taking with me the money for items sold that morning. A tidy sum to add to my bargaining power for when R&F's shutters came down for good. Then, the only thing left to do was to split the money and items remaining on our books. Although I didn't know it at the time, lady luck had taken up residence in my corner. Whilst still awaiting Ray'R and F closing down meeting day.

Driving from Ongar to Brentwood I passed a garage. Tucked away in the far corner of the forecourt was a small cottage, outside of which appeared a free standing one word poster. That one word read ANTIQUES. I was fascinated, never having seen it before. It was Saturday tomorrow, and I had decided to call at the office to catch-up on the latest E3 developments. Finishing early and wanting petrol, I parked and entered the cottage.

There was very little I considered worth a second glance and was about to leave when a voice said, "Did you see anything you liked?" The voice belonged to an elderly lady. She went on to tell me she was leaving Ongar for good. What I could see were part of her own collection she had decided to sell. I told her I was a collector, but of antique, hand painted and transfer printed jugs and mugs. She then told me upstairs she had a hand painted WEEMYS mug with a cockerel chasing hens around its base. She commanded me to stay put as up the stairs she went to retrieve it. She swiftly returned with said mug, telling me a man from London had valued it at £115.00 some three years ago. Would I care to buy it. Buy it? I disliked it and knew nothing about WEEMYS. Except it was Scottish and I had no intention of buying it. So, I told her I'd give it some thought and let her know.

I thought no more about it as I drove home. Pat told me she had collected my monthly Antique magazine. I poured myself a cold beer, picked up my magazine and climbed into my comfortable armchair. Now I must ask the question. Do you believe in miracles? As I turned to the contents page, one word stood out from the rest. WEEMYS! There it was. A four-page article on the short-lived Scottish manufacturer of quality hand painted mugs/jugs. Plus, a whole range of collectible eighteenth/nineteenth century pots. As I read it, each informative page made exciting reading. However, WEEMYS' business life was short lived, and its product range rejected by the Scots. Consequently, a very large percentage of WEEMYS adventurous output made its way south. And glory be. I knew the whereabouts of a hand painted mug, complete with a randy cockerel chasing three teasing hens.

Now, over one hundred years later, the Scots were intent on recovering every piece of renegade WEEMYS pottery to its rightful homeland. Whatever the price! But. Best of all. Christie's, the world-famous London Auctioneers organise a yearly WEEMYS Spring auction at St. Andrews Golf Club. Before returning to the Ongar cottage, I confirmed with Christie's the next Scottish WEEMYS Auction was to be held in the coming April. And yes, St. Andrews Golf Club was the venue. On Monday, Eva (the cottage lady's name) was surprised to see me so soon after my initial visit. I explained, simply out of interest, I researched the mug, liked what I read and decided it would sit comfortably with my sixty-seven other antique mug collection.

I left her £115.00 richer and sat on the train to London, clutching her mug, now soon to be a Christie's exhibit. On inspection, they found a small hairline crack under the mug handle but said it would not affect the price asked. They were right and it sold for a fraction short of £800.00. I told Ray of my good fortune. It bought tears to his eyes at the end of sharing what remained of R&F items. He said he would sue me. I told him I would enjoy spending every pound. Eight hundred times over. This time, the tears were real. And I had substantial funds to buy what and when I wanted to add to my collection.

Chapter Seventeen

There is a greater likelihood of Accrington Stanley winning the Premier League Championship than discovering a football fan who professes to like referees. Unless of course it's another referee. Opinions vary. But collectively they are classified as public enemy number one. Friendless. Hard of Hearing. Blinkered Visionaries. White Stick Blind. Of Doubtful Parentage. A Figure of Fun. To Be Provoked. Decisions Challenged. Authority Questioned. Long before he leaves the dressing room he knows, no matter how well he controls the game, he has made more enemies than friends.

I qualified as a referee in 1968. Like so many Referees I've known in the twenty odd years since "de-peaing "my whistle. The stories I've collected you wouldn't believe. Nor will you the collective of articles hurled onto the pitch and at me during matches. By ignorant spectators who, if they knew the rules governing the game, would be aghast at their own idiotic behaviour.

I realised that each time I officiated, my life was endangered. And why was that? Because, as shared with you previously, my youngest son, Christopher, then an eight-year-old Scout Cub had laid an ambush into which I had innocently walked, unknowingly.

One of my greatest regrets was not pursuing a journalistic career. Especially when my belief that I would return to the Sunday Pictorial (now the Sunday Mirror) was shattered. When I left the Royal Air Force after National Service. I had forever believed I was destined to be a journalist, but the job they offered was in circulation. My answer was thanks, but no thanks. Instead, I ventured into advertising sales, on a series of different trade publications. Many years later, I became the Managing Director of an Essex based small rural graphics studio. My remit was to develop Shape into a small but fully fledged Advertising Agency, which I did. In the thirteenth month as Managing Director of Shape, our billing had reached one point two five million pounds. My colleagues accused me of walking on water. But only at low tide.

Once again, lady luck appeared on my radar. You will recall earlier I explained buying an increasing amount of creativity from a studio. Shape by name, for my accounts now with Beacon. I had informed them of my growing concerns with JD. And how it would probably affect the amount of creative work, Grace (one of my employees) and I had regularly sent to them. Unbeknown to me they had recently had a series of evening meetings discussing the development of Shape's future. They were a limited company, and all six employees were equal share holding directors. One, Ian McGowan, had an elder brother John.

When I was a publisher with McLean Hunter, I employed John as an advertising salesman. He was good when he worked but only worked when it suited him. Eventually I was advised to get rid of him, which I did. But not before he had Introduced me to brother Ian and Shape. We maintained contact and when he arranged a presentation which Grace and I attended. JD was also invited. He accepted. Then went on holiday. Bloody rude I thought, but Grace and I were most impressed. From that moment in time, I became increasingly unhappy with the basic creativity our own studio produced. No matter who the clients were. Grace and I, together with one other in-house account executive, commenced briefing Shape artists. They immediately produced creative advertising campaigns, praised, and accepted by clients.

The Shape team were aware of this, and unbeknown to me decided to approach me to join them. This was agreed on a four to two vote, as I was to discover when asked to attend an evening meeting in Ingatestone. The two directors against offering me the opportunity of joining were not present. However, they made it clear should I join, both would leave. The offer was accepted, and I left for home well pleased with the terms. Especially the title of Managing Director of Shape Advertising and Publicity Limited. The expectation of my new fellow directors was that Shape would be a recognised rural advertising agency within three years.

Chapter Eighteen

Regarding my promotion, it came with an unexpected shock. Unbeknown to me, or any of my family, Nicky, my daughter was confronted with a close to death Irish Wolfhound. Delivered to her vets in Blackmore by the local police. By the name of Kylie, she weighed just 56lbs. It should have been eight stone. Her left eye socket was empty. Her eye missing. So too was her coat, leaving her whole body exposed and covered in sores. All nails on her front paws were much overgrown. Making every step taken extremely painful.

Nicky told me at first sight she and her fellow vet nurses burst into tears. She noticed the police who had rushed her to the vets were close to tears too. Telling how a man had taken Kylie to the police station, explained to all and sundry present that he had found her in the front garden. Already incensed by the description given, the following day I dropped into the vets to see this 'near to death' bitch. The tears came once she entered the room.

The same day Nicky contacted a good friend and RSPCA officer.

Together they tried to arrange a meeting, with the man they believed to be her rightful owner. The same man who took her to the police, saying he found her in his garden. They couldn't because he wouldn't. They then contacted his next-door neighbour. This time successfully. But in a

Pub, not their house. They had not been on speaking terms for a long time. They said he was a rough diamond. On the information given, the RSPCA issued a Court Summons. It said Kylie was never allowed in the house. No matter the weather, she lived outdoors. They rarely saw her fed. But, on more than one occasion saw her, with loaves of plastic wrapped bread, running home from the high street. Hunger turned this beautiful creature into a thief. The neighbours willingly gave the RSPCA a written statement, saying they were willing to appear in court, if required.

Having ignored the summons by not appearing at court on the day his case was due to be heard. A warrant was immediately issued for his arrest. The charges were cruelty, neglect and starvation. Charges he could neither deny nor ignore. He further admitted to keeping another dog. A fully grown GSD upon whom he lavished all his affection. Unlike Kylie, it lived in the house, well loved and cared for. In its summing up, the court forbade him from keeping animals for ten years - what happened to the GSD I know not. He was also fined the pitiful sum of eighty pounds. All of us involved believed it to be totally inadequate. Kylie however was making a remarkable recovery. When first seen by Nicky, my daughter, she weighed a shade under four stone. She should have weighed at least eight plus. Each day, she came closer to her true weight, with her re-grown coat already covering her resurrected frame. With not a sign of apses to be seen anywhere. Sadly, her left eye socket remained empty. This all happened during the 1989-1992 recession. Believed to be the worst on record. Try as they did, the vets found it impossible to re-home her, being such a large dog. Driving home from Ongar, I had no idea what lie in wait. I bet however you, the readers, do.

As I pulled onto our drive, having stopped for my customary pint, Nicky appeared in my headlights. "Leave the car, dad," she said. "I'll put it away for you." Awaiting me in the house was a very large, comforting Bloody Mary. Now my suspicions were aroused. Nicky denied there was anything amiss when I questioned her. Pat said my suspicions were unfounded. So, I had my dinner and settled in front of the TV. Come morning, my car was still on the drive. When I asked why, I was told there was no room for yet another large object in there. "Go see for yourself," said Nicky, "I'm off to work." I gently opened the garage back door, only to be confronted by a huge, hairy, tongue lolling, excitable and kennelled Kylie. "Looks like she's come to stay," said Pat, who'd followed me into the garage.

We already had four rescued waifs living with us. Would one more make any difference? Kylie did. She brought so much joy into my life. Outside of me, she chose the Jack Russell as her canine next of kin. They were inseparable and a joy to watch playing together. I used to watch our re-born new inmate bounding round Hylands Park like a rocking horse. On her way back, when she thought the elderly Jack Russell was tiring, she gently nudged her back to the car. Then tragedy struck. She was diagnosed with terminal cancer. I was diagnosed with heart rending sadness.

We were well towards the end of three years together. As ever I went into the lounge to say my usual good morning to Kylie. But instead of bounding across the lounge to greet me, she lifted her head but remained in her bed. Where it had been, there was a noticeable pool of mucus. Knowing the first six cruel years of her existence, alarm bells started to ring. Appointment made, later that afternoon I was on my way to the vets. They asked me to leave her overnight and she would be examined by a cancer specialist in the morning. The result. An inoperable head tumour. Kylie was given a maximum 10-12 weeks to live. The whole family were shattered. I was in pieces.

For the next nine weeks, she never once left my side. She even vacated her own basket in the utility room, to sleep next to me on the bedroom floor. There was no doubt in my mind. Kylie knew she was dying. As the weeks passed, she grew weaker, whilst the muzzle mucus grew stronger. I think she knew her time had come. By now I was sitting on the floor with her. Her head on my lap. She chose to lay on her left side. Enabling her remaining single eye to gaze, unwaveringly and full of despair, upon my face. In her dying moments, I could see the tears forming. She was trying weakly to say her last goodbye in the only way she could. People say big boys don't cry. They do. I did. Just then, the vet arrived to put her to sleep. Too late, she was at peace. Gone. Wherever canines go when they die. This was her epitaph when we buried her ashes at Pets at Rest.

Kylie's Epitaph
I stood beside your bed last night, you found it hard to sleep
I wiped away a silent tear and begged you not to weep
I whispered to you softly, I'm with you have no fear
I haven't really left you, I'm well, I'm fine, I'm here
I was close to you at breakfast, but that you could not see
Thinking of the many times your hand reached down to me
I was with you at my grave today, you tend it with such care
How can I reassure you; I'm not really lying there?
It's possible for me to be so close to you today
If only I could let you know I never went away
You sat there very quietly; you smiled as if you knew
In the stillness of each evening, I'm so very close to you.
And when the time is right for you, to cross that brief divide
I'll be waiting there to greet you, never more to leave your side.
Sadly, Kylie we must part, I'll carry you for ever in my heart.

Chapter Nineteen

You will have noticed throughout the book; I have always kept lady luck on my radar. I believed she stayed very close to me in every aspect of my life to the present day. All but for one very important area of living. My health. It's here, from the early sixties to the present day, she deserted me. Left alone to fight the dreaded big 'C'. Not once, but three times. For even now, I am still fighting the last vestige of skin cancer. The third of three long visits when, uninvited, cancers came calling. The first, Prostate Cancer which, once I had enlisted the help of radiotherapy and Broomfield Hospital, was a battle won. It took time, and once confirmed the cancer was positive, radiotherapy treatment began, accompanied by hormone injections.

In the interim years, and apart from being declared a Diabetic 2 which, in the latter years, has proved a damn sight more demanding than any of my three cancers. In fact, as I entered my early sixties, I totally ignored what was happening down below. Which was silly really, having already kicked cancer into touch once. Admitted, it was a long time ago and problems occurring were not the same. It really was a case of once bitten twice shy. But I was wrong and cancer two, having been given the freedom of my bladder, had been beavering quietly away. Unheralded, unnoticed, and most definitely, uninvited. All was revealed when I reported to Colchester Hospital for my six-monthly Prostrate cancer check-up.

It All Kicks Off On Sunday

As ever, once again the report was fine. This, and the Consultant involved fully expected my Prostate to pass inspection. It did, but having revealed of late when urinating, I was experiencing a burning sensation. And how the discomfort was increasing. He immediately arranged an urgent appointment for six days hence. This involved passing a tube down through my 'todger', which had a minute camera attached. Once inside my bladder it went walkabout. I was invited to join in and look at the l large screen to my left. I was now able to see inside my own bladder. How many of you can say that? As I joined the consultant in "hunt the felon," we both saw it at the same time. I would have probably missed it in the excitement. But the Consultant was onto it immediately. "Sorry old son," he said, "we've a new fight on our hands, starting today. You've got bladder cancer."

I was truly gobsmacked. Prostate cancer was a nasty shock. But here was I. Facing another fight, the outcome of which, once again was out of my hands. I straightway started on the course of BCG treatment. Prescribed for bladder cancer and to start immediately. This entailed visits to Colchester Hospital. Where that all too familiar tube, camera attachment with BCG medication, confronted man's best friend. This was preferred to surgery. I was glad as I had a lifetime dread of going under the knife. Bladder cancer was the confirmed opinion of all involved. It should have been problem free. It wasn't.

Let me explain how the medication was administered. Asked to be treated early and was. Every week I arrived at the hospital at 8a.m. Removed my lower garments and was positioned lying on my back alongside a large screen. I had never previously exposed my privates to four people at the same time. Here I had no option. Three were nurses. All wearing white gloves. The senior nurse advanced, the hateful tube held in her left hand. The mere sight of it gave my 'todger' the tremors. From standing proud in her right hand, it collapsed into a pile of five facile wrinkles. Of no use to man or beast. And very difficult in which to insert the tube and its medical cargo.

After six doses of BCG, I was feeling quite pleased with how well the treatment was progressing. For six-weekly 8am BCG dosage appointments, all was well. Then disaster struck. When producing my required sample, it was heavily blooded. So much so, just one look and a doctor was alerted. I was sent home with no BCG tubed into my bladder. We were both most disappointed as this went on for seven weeks. It ended with my seeking a second opinion and my case being transferred to a London Hospital. But with the understanding no other hospitals were to be involved.

Three years later, all sign of the big C had disappeared. I now have yearly appointments, during which I am granted a reunion with the inside of my bladder. I thought that was cancer finally banished. Never to return. Once again, I was wrong. I am now battling with skin cancer. This has meant surgery to remove it totally from a large area of my scalp. Accompanied with a sizeable piece of skin, removed from my leg, and then grafted onto the area of surgery. Now I must wait to see if the plastic surgery operation has completely banished the third cancer attack on my person, having decided enough is enough. As all my cancer treatments over many years have been - except the last - by daily hospital appointments. Never once did it interfere with my football or refereeing activities.

As I said, right from the very beginning, like so many, I fell in love with the beautiful game. That has never changed. Even though there are those doing their level best to impose their ideas, their money, their demands upon changing football as true fans know it. In my forty plus years as a referee, I fought long and hard to maintain all that was good in the game. Sadly, each season the 'suits' use their money. Inevitably changes result and football suffers the consequences.

I believe it started in earnest in 1961, when the then "capped" player wages of £20 weekly were scrapped. Immediately Johnny Haynes, Fulham and England striker, asked for and was given the then unheard-of increase to £100.00 each and every week. Later, the rule that limited the number of foreign players signed per club to one. Soon increased to three, before being cancelled all together. Now football, especially the Premiership, is awash with players from around the world. I understand in 2022, individual wages, loaded with bonus earnings, reached half a million weekly. Also, the number of black professional footballers playing for English clubs totals forty-three percent. This year, Manchester City signed a Norwegian striker playing in Germany. The signing on fee was sixty million pounds. His weekly wage. An immoral four hundred thousand pounds weekly. This then topped by Ronaldo. Contracted by Manchester United at £500.000 weekly. Bloody ridiculous. No wonder when Dad takes his son to a game, buys him an ice cream or burger, the dent in his wallet often means he doesn't do it often. Ex-premiership and England six-foot seven-inch retired striker Peter Crouch wrote an article. Published in the Daily Mail, titled Save Our Beautiful Game. Read it and you would think whilst he held the pen, I held his hand. I am in full agreement with all he had to say.

Chapter Twenty

The final chapter I consider to be a feat of human endurance. It concerns Pat and her permanent desire to entice Mr. Brock and friends into our large back garden. Our new home was surrounded on three sides by an orchard. Pat approached the owners seeking permission to walk the dogs (we had five rescued dogs living with us at that time) in the orchard. Permission given; Pat saw the tell-tale signs that Badgers had set up homes. Being inquisitive, she asked Steve how many. His reply was sixty-five on the last survey carried out three years previously. She immediately began to plan how to entice them into our garden.

I was commanded to make a floor level opening through the hawthorn hedge. This done, Pat had read somewhere that Badgers had a sweet tooth. And so, it began. Every other day, she spent, preparing the Badgers supper. I could not believe its content. There were sandwiches of strawberry jam, chocolate spread, Marmite, and cheese spread. All beautifully quartered. Rich Tea and digestive biscuits. I honestly thought the Vicar was coming to tea.

As soon as it was dark, we took this regal feast into the garden. I was instructed to place the goodies at the hole in the hedge. Then lay a path of the same to a position where we could clearly see the remainder of the Badgers' supper. We then returned indoors and took up our viewing positions. It was nine o'clock and we waited. It was midnight and we waited. There was not a sign of Mr. Brock. After a week of night vigilance, there was still nary a sign of a Badger. We chased away a fox on two occasions. By now, we were wondering if we were ever going to see our prey. By the tenth night I'd had enough. I told Pat I'd had enough. No more late nights for me. But still she watched. Often well into the wee small hours. It was the end of week three. I had only just gone to bed when I was roughly shaken and woken. Pat was standing over me, "Come quickly, we've got our first badger." I rushed into the lounge and there he was. Mr. Brock. Paying a long-awaited visit to Pat's sandwich bar. Pat could not tear herself away from the window. Willing our badger to return. Pat continued to put out the nightly fare. It remained untouched for a week. She was deeply disappointed, but convinced our Badger would return. And he did, but this time accompanied by his or her mate. All Pat's dreams coming true. But neither of us could imagine from one small Badger, in the third year there were now ELEVEN Badgers. Any fear of humans had long since disappeared.

Any time we were late with their supper, they would come onto the Patio. Then either sit or lie until Pat appeared with the food. Latterly, we would go into the garden and stand twenty feet from their lawn table, they were happy with our presence. I swear Pat could feed them by hand. She agreed but would not do so for fear of spooking them, never to return. Believe it or not, we had people from the Midlands. They would ring and ask if they could come and take photos. We were also most popular with our neighbours and people who had only seen dead badgers by the roadside.

Unexpectedly, we were confronted by a new Bank manager. One of the new brigades who refused to continue to support our sizeable overdraft. He was an arrogant bugger, who left me with no other option than to sell the house. We did, to a couple with two daughters. Each had their own horse. He wanted both to become proficient equestrians. Within a month he had converted one acre of paddock into a menage. Not how Pat and I had envisaged leaving the Badgers if and when we had to sell the house. Because we were forced to sell the house, we stopped feeding the Badgers. They couldn't fathom why the food had stopped. I was sad watching them leave in ones and twos. Pat was deeply upset as the last Badger left. It was the end of an era for us both. I know Pat will carry a multitude of memories in her heart. As for me, it is a fitting ending for my book and a fond farewell to my readers.

Milton Keynes UK
Ingram Content Group UK Ltd.
UKHW020056091223
434043UK00014B/650